J. W. (Judson Wade) Bishop

The Story of a Regiment

Being a Narrative of the Service of the second Regiment, Minnesota Veteran

Volunteer Infantry, in the Civil War of 1861-1865

J. W. (Judson Wade) Bishop

The Story of a Regiment
Being a Narrative of the Service of the second Regiment, Minnesota Veteran Volunteer Infantry, in the Civil War of 1861-1865

ISBN/EAN: 9783337116484

Printed in Europe, USA, Canada, Australia, Japan

Cover: Foto ©ninafisch / pixelio.de

More available books at **www.hansebooks.com**

THE
STORY OF A REGIMENT

BEING A NARRATIVE OF THE

Service of the Second Regiment,

MINNESOTA VETERAN VOLUNTEER
INFANTRY,

IN THE CIVIL WAR OF 1861-1865,

BY

JUDSON W. BISHOP.

(LATE COLONEL AND BVT. BRIG. GENL. U. S. A.)

WRITTEN AND PUBLISHED FOR, AND BY REQUEST OF THE
SURVIVING MEMBERS OF THE REGIMENT.

ST. PAUL, MINN.
1890.

Presented to

with the Compliments of the Author

Entered according to act of Congress, in the year 1890, by J. W. Bishop, in the office of the Librarian of Congress, at Washington.

INTRODUCTION.

In response to the often repeated request of my comrades, now surviving, of the Second Minnesota Regiment, I recently promised to write a connected narrative of the service of the regiment from 1861 to 1865.

Having been the first man to be mustered into that regiment and the last man to be mustered out of it, and having served continuously in it from first to last, and having for more than half the term of service, had the responsibility of its administration, discipline and command, it should not be a difficult task for me to make a continuous record of all important events in its history. As moreover its services were always and everywhere honorable, efficient and satisfactory, it should be, and is, a labor of love to review and record them.

But amid the absorbing and varied cares of a busy life I have found it impossible to give to the work the continuous attention that is necessary to perform such work well, and I should not be satisfied with it now, if I could suppose that I should ever have the leisure time in which to improve upon it.

It is intended to be and I believe is, a faithful and truthful record of facts and events, and as such will be tested without discredit by the official reports and the diaries and letters of the time With less care in this respect, and with more freedom of invention and imagination, a more interesting and readable war story could doubtless have been made of it.

In writing the story of the regiment the frequent mention of names has been avoided. A great many of the seventeen hundred and eighty men who were members of it have well deserved personal mention for gallant and meritorious conduct, else the regiment as such could not have acquired its conceded high reputation, but it is obviously impossible to mention all, or some without omitting others equally worthy, and my comrades generally will, I trust, be content to claim the history of the regiment, which they helped to make, as their own, and be proud of it as they have a right to be.

A part of the record history of the regiment consists of such correspondence, official reports, orders and recommendations as would encumber the progress of the narrative if placed therein; these are given in the appendix, usually in full, and from official sources. Some of them are now for the first time in print and all of them will be of interest to members of the regiment.

I had proposed to append also a complete roster giving the official military record of each and all the members of the regiment, but I find upon examination, that the only record thus far compiled is imperfect, erroneous and unsatisfactory. The compilation of a new and complete one from original rolls and records is impracticable within the time at my command, and I am thus compelled to close the book without it.

This is less to be regretted, however, in view of the fact that the State has by law provided for the preparation of an official roster of all the Minnesota soldiers, of which every such soldier now surviving (or his representative if dead) is to receive a copy free of expense.

I am under obligations to comrades D. C. Wilson, Wm. Bircher and M. D. E. Runals for the use of their daily journals (1861 to 1865) which have been valuable references in locating events and dates.

The work, such as it is, Comrades, is now submitted in the hope that it will meet your kind approval and that it may revive, as you read it, your interest and pride in the memory of our regiment and of your service in and with it, as it has indeed revived mine to prepare the record for you.

J. W. BISHOP.

St. Paul, June, 1890.

CONTENTS.

PAGE.

CHAPTER I.—GETTING INTO THE SERVICE.................... 17

 The war opens at Sumpter—The President's call for troops—Gov. Ramsey tenders a regiment—The executive proclamation—The Adjutant General's order—The militia companies—Company "A" holds a meeting—And volunteers—And is formally tendered—And accepted for the 1st regiment—Is afterwards left out as supernumerary—And awaits a call for a second regiment—Marching orders received—The company re-enlists for three years—Reports at Fort Snelling—Is mustered into the service—Marches to Fort Ripley—Other companies report and are mustered in—Field and staff officers are appointed—Regiment assembled at Fort Snelling—Preparations for going South—Mrs. and Miss Van Cleve.

CHAPTER II.—GOING TO THE WAR...................... 26

 We leave Fort Snelling—The march through St. Paul—Voyage down the river—La Crosse—Chicago and the "Wigwam"—Our Pittsburg Reception—Orders changed—A voyage down the Ohio river—Louisville, Kentucky—A call on Gen. Sherman—A night ride to Lebanon Junction—Assigned to Gen. Geo. H. Thomas' division—Relieved by 3rd Minnesota regiment—Ordered to Lebanon—Brigaded with other regiments—The mules and the wagoners.

CHAPTER III.—THE MILL SPRINGS CAMPAIGN............ 33

 Our march out on New Year's day—Leaving the "pike"—Rain, mud and discomfort—Only the top rail—Apple jack—Logan's cross roads—Topography—Assembling the troops—Out on picket—The night before the battle—The attack upon the pickets—Long roll in the camps—The battle opens—The 2nd Minnesota goes in—The fighting "through the same fence"—Killing of Bailie Peyton—A bayonet charge—Hon. Charles Scheffer—Death of Gen. Zollicoffer—The enemy routed—Our pursuit—Bivouac on Moulden's Hill—We occupy the enemy's camp next morning—Captured artillery, animals and stores—Battle flag captured by 2nd Minnesota—Killed and wounded.

CHAPTER IV.—MILL SPRINGS TO SHILOH 49

Return march to Louisville—Dr. Jackson's farm—A flag presented by the loyal ladies of Louisville—Voyage down the Ohio river to Smithfield—And up the Cumberland to Nashville—March from Nashville—Detention at Duck river—Rain, mud and night marching—Arrival at Savannah—By river to Shiloh—The battle field—Burial of the dead—Col. VanCleve promoted—Band mustered out—Halleck's arrival—Seige of Corinth—Evacuation, and pursuit of the enemy—Disappointment and disgust.

CHAPTER V.—CORINTH TO LOUISVILLE 57

Our march eastward—Camp at Tuscumbia—Fourth of July—Gov. Ramsey's visit—The "bugle band" organized—Florence—Sensational proceedings in church—"Kingdom Comin"—The plundering of Athens, Tennessee—The murder of Gen. Robert L. McCook—Company "C" 3rd Minnesota regiment—News of the Indian massacre in Minnesota—Lieut. Col. Wilkin appointed Colonel of 9th Minnesota regiment—March to Nashville—Bragg's army crosses the Cumberland—The race for Louisville—Seventy miles in three days—"Sink holes" and "dough gods"—The battle of the apples—Cave

City—A hard march via Elizabethtown to the Ohio river at the mouth of Salt river—Steamers to Louisville—Orders relieving Buell issued and suspended.

CHAPTER VI.—THE PERRYVILLE CAMPAIGN............... 69
Killing of Gen. William Nelson—Reorganization of of the army—Capt. Gilbert and Capt. Gay assigned to command over their seniors—We march out to find the enemy—A seventeen mile skirmish—The battle of Perryville—Our brigade ordered in at twilight—A startling experience—Comments on the battle—The pursuit to Crab Orchard—A cocky Inspector General—An arrest ordered and trouble promised—Crab Orchard via Lebanon, Cave City and Bowling Green to Mitchelville—Repairing the tunnel—Camp at Cunningham's Ford—Capture of new regiments—Gallatin, Tennessee—Proclamation of Emancipation—A lard mine—Ordered to rejoin the division.

CHAPTER VII.—TRIUNE AND TULLAHOMA.................. 80
A vain chase after Wheeler's cavalry—Camp at the Battle farm—The Battle family—An inspection of the regiment—Col. George goes to Minnesota—A brilliant fight by our foraging party—Congratulatory orders—Good-by to the Battle family—An expedition to Harpeth river—A quick march to Chapel Hill—A fight and capture of prisoners—Encampment at Triune—Building fortifications—Our detail samples Gen. Steedman's whiskey—We get Enfield rifles—Gen. Schofield succeeds Steedman, and Gen. Brannan succeeds Schofield in the command of the division—Brigade exercises—"Pup tents" issued—A grand review—A night march to Franklin—An inhospitable reception—Tullahoma campaign begins—A rainy day skirmish—An astonished surgeon—Hoover's Gap—Tullahoma captured—Fording Elk river.

CHAPTER VIII.—THE CAMPAIGN AND BATTLE OF
CHICAMAUGA... 91

Up the Cumberland mountains—An adjourned university—Battle Creek—Picketing the Tennessee river—Building rafts and scows—Crossing the river—Nic-a-Jack Cave—Crossing Racoon mountain—Lookout Valley—Lookout Mountain—Lee's Mill—A scrimmage at Pond Springs—The night march before the battle—That breakfast we never ate—The opening of Chicamauga—Our first day's battle—The stampeded brigade—Charge of the 9th Ohio—Desperate fighting of our brigade—Final repulse of the enemy—Next day in reserve—The skulkers—The wounded general officer—Ordered to the left flank—Fight with Breckenridge's division—Change of front under fire—Dispersion of the enemy—Snodgrass Hill—Gen. Thomas—A memorable afternoon—Our successful defense of the ridge—Withdrawal to Rossville at night—Every man accounted for—Our brigade commander's report—Heavy loss of our brigade.

CHAPTER IX.—CHATTANOOGA AND MISSION RIDGE......113

Establishing the parallel camps in line of battle—Scanty supply of food, forage and clothing—Our diversions "such as they were"—Skirmishing for fuel—The big guns on Lookout—Reorganization—Col. George is again compelled to leave us—Topography of Chattanooga—Enemy signalling over our heads—Opening of the "Cracker line"—Preparations for the grand battle—Hooker's battle above the clouds—Sherman's attack on Mission Ridge—Grand and successful assault on Mission Ridge by the Army of the Cumberland—Official report of our regimental commander—Movements of our brigade and of our regiment deployed in the front—Capture of the first line of breastworks—Our brigade commander commends the 2nd Minnesota—Comments on the battle.

CHAPTER X.—VETERANIZING..................................128

Return to Chattanooga—Burying the Chicamauga dead—Invited to reinlist—Discussion in the camps—Eighty per cent decide favorably, and are re-enlisted as veterans—The non-veterans are detached—The regiment starts for Minnesota—Steamers to Bridgeport—Box cars to Nashville—And thence to Louisville—The freedom of the city claimed and granted for the veterans—Our old muskets turned in—A memorable ride to Chicago—That breakfast at Crawfordsville—The sleigh ride from La Crosse to St. Paul—Hospitality of Winona people—Warm reception of the veterans at St. Paul—The veteran furlough—Public reception at Chatfield—Address by the regimental commander—Reassembling at Fort Snelling—Our entertainment by the ladies of St. Anthony—Return by stages to La Crosse—Col. George rejoins here and assumes command—By rail to Nashville—March thence to Bridgeport—Rejoin division at Ringgold, Georgia.

CHAPTER XI.—THE ATLANTA CAMPAIGN....................142

Stripping for work—Reconnoisance—The campaign begins—Tunnel Hill—Snake Creek Gap—Dalton, then Resaca, evacuated—Calhoun—Cassville—The 9th Ohio goes home—The famous "hundred days"—Intrenching a line under fire—A battery comes into action—Lieut. Jones killed—Gen. Howard's account of it—Kenesaw mountain—An unrestful camp—A moonlight march—A sad event—Col. George and our non-veterans mustered out—Unsuccessful assault of Davis' division—Kenesaw evacuated—Recruits arrive—Garrison duty at Marietta—Again to the front—More recruits—Back to Marietta—Post and Garrison duty—Again to the front—Battle of Jonesboro—Atlanta evacuated—Force and casualties report—An unpleasant history—Gen. Thomas requests the Governor to fill up the regiment—Lieut. Col. Bishop sent to Minnesota for the recruits—And returns—Hood's army in our rear and our pursuit—Silver horns for the band—Return to Atlanta.

CHAPTER XII.—THE MARCH TO THE SEA..................156

The burning of Atlanta—Our march out eastward—Unbuilding the railroad—An unfortunate train—A resurrection—Howell Cobb's farm—Milledgeville—A provisional legislature—Repeal of the Ordinance of Secession—The foragers and their methods—No straggling allowed—A Methodist minister among the conscripts—"See that you fall not out by the way"—After the enemy's cavalry—Rice with the bark on—A foraging expedition—Fort McAllister falls—Supplies from the fleet—Savannah evacuated—40 days' mail—Irish potatoes—Christmas and fresh oysters—Chaplain Gleason—Grand review in Savannah—Our regiment ordered into the city—In charge of Central railroad grounds and property—Maj. Uline sent to Minnesota for recruits.

CHAPTER XIII.—SAVANNAH TO RALEIGH.....................168

The campaign of the Carolinas—We leave Savannah—Sister's Ferry—Cross the river into South Carolina—Devastation of the country—Barnwell Court House—Destroying the railroad—Pontooning the river—The country on fire—Burning of Columbia—Sunday work—The Catawba river—A precarious crossing—Hanging Rock battle ground—The Great Pedee river—Cross into North Carolina—A burning stream—Fayetteville—Destruction of the arsenal—Battle of Bentonville—Arrival at Goldsboro—An impromptu review—60 days' mail at once—A military execution—An inspection—The band—Maj. Uline returns—Some promotions—News of Lee's surrender—Advance to Raleigh—State Insane Asylum—Johnston's surrender—Halleck's discourtesy towards Sherman.

PAGE.

CHAPTER XIV.—RICHMOND, WASHINGTON AND HOME..181

"A comfortable and leisurely march"—A race of the 14th and 20th corps—We cross into Virginia—Our arrival at Richmond—Forbidden to enter the city—Gen. Halleck proposes to review the 14th corps—Sherman countermands it—And orders our march to Washington—We "route step" through Richmond—The Chicahominy—Pamunkey—Rapidan and Rappahannock rivers—Bristoe station—Manassas and Bull Run battle fields—Alexandria—The grand review in Washington—A magnificent military spectacle—Change of encampment—A visit and review by Gen. Geo. H. Thomas—Reorganization of our division—Col. Bishop assigned to command the 1st brigade—Voyage down the Ohio river—Encampment at Louisville—20 days of suspense—Muster for discharge—Farewell orders and addresses by our division and corps commanders—By rail to Chicago and La Crosse—Steamer to Fort Snelling—A parade march at Winona—Grand reception at St. Paul—Encamp at Fort Snelling—Farewell address by the Colonel—Final payment and discharge—Dispersion of the men and "good-by."

CHAPTER XV.—CONCLUDING REMARKS..........................192

In the beginning, the inexperience of officers and men—Organization and duty by companies—The regiment becomes later the unit—Brigading by States—The soldier learns how to take care of himself—The evolution of discipline—To be always "present and ready"—Army transportation—"Pup tents"—Regimental Bands—Our "pioneer corps"—Recruiting the veteran regiments—Comparative inefficiency of new regiments—Average good physical condition of the old soldier—They have generally been successful in civil life—And partially because of their military experience and training—The Great Beyond.

APPENDIX.

PAGE

No. 1. Adjutant General's order (State of Minnesota) to captains of militia companies. April 17th, 1861...203

No. 2. Acceptance (telegram) of Company "A" by Lieut. Gov. Ignatius Donnelly. April 22nd, 1861....203

No. 3. Acceptance (letter) of Company "A" by Lieut. Gov. Ignatius Donnelly. April 22nd, 1861...............203

No. 4. Order by John B. Sanborn, Adjutant General, to Company "A" to turn over the arms and equipments for companies of the 1st regiment. April 26th, 1861...204

No. 5. Tender of "Chatfield Guards" as unconditional volunteers. May 4th, 1861.................................204

No. 6. Application of "Chatfield Guards" for reissue of arms and equipments. June 7th, 1861...............204

No. 7. Orders from Adjutant General's office to designate the post commander at Fort Snelling. June 26th, 1861...205

No. 8. Gen. Geo. H. Thomas' report transmitting a rebel flag, captured by 2nd Minnesota regiment at Mill Springs. Dated February 3rd, 1862...............205

No. 9. Report of battle of Mill Springs, by Col. H. P. Van Cleve, commanding 2nd regiment Minnesota volunteers. Dated January 22nd, 1862.................206

INDEX TO APPENDIX.   13

                                                                    PAGE.
No. 10. Official list of killed and wounded of 2nd Minnesota regiment at battle of Mill Springs. (12 killed and 33 wounded.) 207

No. 11. Report of battle of Mill Springs, by Col. Robert L. McCook, commanding 3rd brigade, 1st division. Dated January 27th, 1862 208

No. 12. Report of battle of Mill Springs, by Gen. George H. Thomas, commanding 1st division. Dated January 31st, 1862 211

No. 13. Gen. W. S. Rosecrans' order commending the 2nd Minnesota regiment (after inspection by Capt. James Curtis) as "worthy of imitation" 215

No. 14. Complimentary order by Col. Van Derveer, commanding 3rd brigade, commending the gallant conduct of Sergant L. N. Holmes and fourteen men of Company "H" in repulsing an attack of rebel calvary. Dated February, 1863 215

No. 15. Report (referring to No. 14) of Gen. J. B. Steedman, commanding division. Dated February 15th, 1863 216

No. 16. Report of battle of Chicamauga, by Col. James George, commanding 2nd Minnesota regiment. Dated September 25th, 1863 216

No. 17. Official list of killed, wounded and captured of the 2nd Minnesota regiment at battles of Chicamauga. (Killed 35, wounded 113, captured 14; total loss, 162.) 219

No. 18. Supplementary report of Col. James George, commanding 2nd Minnesota regiment, commending certain officers and men, "for gallant and meritorious conduct." Dated September 30th, 1863 223

No. 19. Report of battles of Chicamauga, by Col. F. Van Derveer, commanding 3rd brigade. Dated September 25th, 1863 225

PAGE.

No. 20. Col. James George recommended for promotion...232

No. 21. Official list of killed and wounded of the 2nd Minnesota regiment in battles of Mission Ridge. (Killed 5, wounded 34.)..233

No. 22. Supplementary report of battle of Mission Ridge, by Lieut. Col. J. W. Bishop, commanding 2nd Minnesota regiment. Dated December 10th, 1863..235

No. 23. Report of battle of Mission Ridge, by Col. Van Derveer, commanding 3rd brigade................237

No. 24. Regimental promotions recommended by brigade, division, corps and department commanders. Dated July 14, 1864......................................241

No. 25. Official report of killed and wounded of 2nd Minnesota regiment in Atlanta campaign. (Killed 4, wounded 30.)...242

No. 26. Complimentary letter from Gen. A. Baird, commanding division, to Hon. S. Miller, Governor of Minnesota, commending 2nd Minnesota regiment, and asking for recruits to fill up the regiment.243

No. 27. Report of force and casualties of 2nd Minnesota regiment in the campaign of the Carolinas. (Wounded 2, captured 5.) Dated March 23rd, 1865.244

No. 28. Gen. Bishop attributes his brevet to Brigadier General to the gallant and soldierly conduct of the 2nd regiment..246

No. 29. The promotion twice recommended and requested by the corps and army commanders............247

No. 30. The 2nd Minnesota regiment reported ready for discharge and requests orders to Fort Snelling, Minnesota..248

No. 31. The Corps Commander's farewell address........249

INDEX TO APPENDIX. 15

                          PAGE.

No. 32. Orders to proceed to Fort Snelling, Minnesota.250

No. 33. Roster of officers when regiment left Minnesota for the South, October, 1861..........................251

No. 34. Roster of officers when regiment veteranized, January, 1864..251

No. 35. Roster of officers at final muster out, July, 1865..252

No. 36. Various statistics of the regiment..................253

No. 37. Reunion letters, (1887), from Col. H. V. N. Boynton, Col. F. Van Derveer, Gen. A. Baird and Gen. W. S. Rosecrans..254

ERROR—See page 58. Gov. Ramsey's visit to Tuscumbia was not on, but a few days after the 4th July, 1862.

THE
SECOND REGIMENT

MINNESOTA VETERAN VOLUNTEER INFANTRY

IN THE

CIVIL WAR OF 1861-1865.

CHAPTER I.

GETTING INTO THE SERVICE.

The surrender and evacuation of Fort Sumter on the morning of Sunday, April 14th, 1861, was followed on Monday, the 15th, by the President's proclamation and call for 75,000 men to serve three months.

In orders from the war department, these were apportioned among the several states not then in open rebellion, in ninety-four regiments of 780 men each, the remainder (1,680 men) to be contributed by the District of Columbia.

Hon. Alex. Ramsey, Governor of Minnesota, being then in Washington, immediately tendered the regiment required from this state, and an executive proclamation, signed by Lieut. Governor Ignatius Donnelly, was published in St. Paul, April 16th. It was accompanied by "Special Order No.

1." Adjutant General's office, State of Minnesota, April 16th, 1861, by Wm. H. Acker, Adjutant General.

This order called for one regiment of ten companies, each of 76 officers and men, and it provided that "the first ten companies so organized and "reported ready for service at this office by their "respective captains will be received, provided that "the several militia companies already organized "will be entitled to the preference for the space of "ten days from this date, upon complying with "the foregoing requirements."

The said companies already organized were named, including Company "A" of Chatfield, Fillmore county, of which the writer was captain, and seven others, located at Mankato, New Ulm, St. Anthony, Clear Water, St. Cloud, St. Paul, and Stillwater respectively. (*Appendix No. 1.*)

There were (in 1861) no railroads in Minnesota and no telegraph lines except the single wire from St. Paul along the river bank to LaCrosse, Wis.

The proclamation and special order, mailed on the 17th were received at Chatfield on the 19th, and published in "The Democrat," on the 20th, with a call for a special meeting of the enrolled members of the "Chatfield Guards," (Company A) to be held at the Armory on Monday evening, April 22nd, to consider the call of the Governor for volunteers.

At this meeting, which was fully attended, the call was presented, with a brief address by the Captain; and by a unanimous vote, he was authorized to offer the company and "to report it organized, armed and ready for marching orders."

This tender and report were forwarded by special messenger the same night to Winona, 35 miles, and thence by telegraph to the Adjutant General. (*No copy of it can now be found.*)

On the 24th, a telegram was received from Lieutenant (and acting) Governor Ignatius Donnelly, accepting the company and instructing it to await marching orders. This was the seventh company accepted for the first regiment, two companies from St. Paul, one from St. Anthony and three others preceding it, having received the call two or three days earlier. A letter confirming the telegram was received on the 25th. (*Appendix Nos. 2 and 3.*)

We were puzzled somewhat by observing that both telegram and letter were dated April 22nd, when our tender of service could not have reached St. Paul until the morning of the 23rd, but satisfied ourselves by presuming that they had actually been written on the 23rd and dated by mistake on the 22nd.

It appeared later that a bogus letter purporting to tender the company, with 63 men, "which number could be increased to the full standard within thirty days," had been sent on the 19th to the Governor by some person as yet unknown, who had forged the Captain's name thereto, and that the telegram and letter of acceptance by Lieut. Governor Donnelly were in fact in reply to this bogus tender of a partial company, while our genuine tender of a full company was not responded to until the 26th, when the following telegram was sent by Adjutant General Sanborn, who had in the mean time succeeded Acker, who had resigned to recruit a company, of which he was later commissioned captain:

"St. Paul, April 26th, 1861.
Capt. J. W. Bishop, Chatfield:

You will keep your ranks full if possible. Eleven full companies have already tendered their services, and if ten of these rendezvous here with full ranks your company cannot be received into this regiment. Some may not answer the order of rendezvous.

John B. Sanborn,
Adjutant General."

Meantime, the company, full to the maximum and with more than thirty supernumeraries, had been busily preparing for a prompt response to the expected "marching orders."

If surprised by the telegram, we were, if possible, more astonished by the arrival on the 29th of a special messenger from the Adjutant General's office, with an order for our guns and equipments, and the verbal information that the regiment had been made up by the acceptance of ten companies, which he explained were more conveniently accessible to the rendezvous at Fort Snelling, than ours. (*Appendix No. 4.*)

The disappointment and indignation with which the order was received did not prevent a prompt compliance with it, and the captain went to St. Paul with his guns and without his company.

The guns were received by the Adjutant General with expressions of appreciation of our promptness in volunteering and regret for our disappointment, but there appeared to be no redress then available, and the captain was obliged to return to his disarmed and disgusted company and dismiss the men with the promise that, if the war should last long enough to call for a second regiment, company "A" should not again get left at home.

After authorizing the offer of their services for any regiment thereafter required, the men went to their homes and resumed their ordinary employments. (Appendix Nos. 5 and 6.)

A letter to Hon. H. M. Rice, then in Washington as senator from Minnesota, brought to the writer a kind reply and assurance that he should have the earliest possible notice of any further call for troops; a promise which was faithfully fulfilled by a telegram received at Chatfield in time to enable him to reach St. Paul a little before the call for a second regiment was received by the governor.

The company was again tendered and accepted, and the marching orders below quoted were requested and received on the spot.

"General Headquarters, State of Minnesota.
St. Paul, June 14th, 1865.

Special Order No. 5.
Capt. Judson W. Bishop, Chatfield, Fillmore county, Minnesota:
You will report your company at Fort Snelling without delay, for the purpose of having the same mustered into the service and pay of the United States.
By order of the Commander in Chief.
John B. Sanborn,
Adjutant General."

Similar orders were requested and obtained by Capt. Bishop for Capt. William Markham, who had a company organized in Olmsted county, which orders were carried by him to Chatfield and sent by special messenger to Capt. Markham at Rochester, reaching him next day.

The war was fairly on now, and the call was for three years' men instead of three months. It required several days of active work to reassemble and reenlist, under the new conditions, enough of the men to make a full company of eighty-three men, the minimum now required. Yet it seems incredible, as we now look back upon it, that so many could and would divest themselves of all impeding business, social and family obligations and restraints, and commit themselves for three years to the then unknown hardships and perils of a soldier's life in time of active service.

When we remember that our then young State sent into the field during the war more than one-seventh of her entire population by the census of 1860, we appreciate the spirit with which every loyal heart responded to "The Union, it must, and shall be preserved."

The enlistments commenced at Chatfield on the 16th of June, and on the morning of the 22nd the company marched up the winding hillside road to the table land east of, and overlooking the village, and there halted for the final adieus.

None who were present will ever forget that hour and experience, and we need not try to describe them to others.

We arrived at Winona, traveling in wagons, the same evening, and went thence by river to Fort Snelling, arriving the next day, June 23rd, and on the 26th were mustered into the service of the United States, by Capt. A. D. Nelson, U. S. A., as

Company "A" of the Second Regiment Minnesota Volunteer Infantry, and the writer was immediately assigned to the command of the Post. (*Appendix No. 7.*)

Captain Markham's company, which had arrived on the 24th from Rochester, was mustered in later in the same day (26th) as Company "B" of the same regiment.

Meantime other companies were being recruited, and during the next few days were mustered in successively, as follows: Company "C" from Dodge county, "D" from Ramsey, "E" from Nicollet, "F" from Washington, "G" from Ramsey and Brown, "H" from Blue Earth, "I" from Goodhue, and "K" recruited at large.

After being partially armed, uniformed and supplied, Company "A" marched out from Fort Snelling on the 3rd day of July with orders to garrison the post at Fort Ripley, 130 miles distant on the upper Mississippi river. This march was made wholly on foot, in seven days, one wagon being allowed us for baggage and rations. This was our first experience on our soldier legs, and to many of the men it was a pretty tough one, but they all came through it in good condition and spirit. Company "F," Capt. John B. Davis, followed us a few days later to Fort Ripley, and Companies "B" and "C" went to Fort Abercrombie on the upper Red river, and Companies "D" and "E" to Fort Ridgely on the upper Minnesota river; the other four companies remained at Fort Snelling, with Capt. A. R. Kiefer of Company "G" as the senior officer in command. Thus located, the next few weeks were devoted to drill and instruction of the men.

On the 22nd of July the Governor appointed H. P. Van Cleve as Colonel, James George as Lieut. Colonel and Simeon Smith as Major. Lieut. Daniel Heaney of Company "B" was appointed Adjutant and Lieut. Wm. Grow, of Company "I," Quartermaster. Two days later Reginald Bingham was appointed Surgeon, Moody C. Tolman, Assistant Surgeon, and Rev. Timothy Cressey, Chaplain. Major Smith was within a few days appointed paymaster in the regular army, and on the 10th of September Capt. Alex. Wilkin, of the First Minnesota Regiment, was appointed Major in the Second, *vice* Smith.

Col. Van Cleve had been an officer in the regular army, and Lieut. Col. George and Major Wilkin had served as volunteer officers in the Mexican war. None of the other officers had ever had any actual military experience in the field as far as is known to the writer.

A band of 20 members was here enlisted and organized, with Michael Esch as leader, and at the expense of the State was equipped with instruments and music.

About the 20th of September, orders were sent out from Regimental Headquarters recalling the detached companies from the several garrisoned posts, and within the first week of October the regiment was for the first time assembled at Fort Snelling, Companies "A" and "F" making, as before, the march of 130 miles in seven days, and on arrival reporting every man "for duty."

Here a few days were devoted to active preparation for going to "the front." Instruction and drill, guard mounts and dress parades, and issues of clothing, equipments, arms and ammunition, made a very busy week of it. As the time for departure approached, our camp was thronged with visitors, some curious to see the evolutions and parades, and some to take leave of their soldier boys, who might never return.

Most of the companies were now full or nearly full to the maximum number (101) and the regiment paraded nearly a thousand officers and men, well equipped, and considering their brief service, well disciplined and instructed, though poorly armed with old muskets of several different kinds and calibres; the best at that time available, we were told, and so they were carried without complaint until opportunity should arrive to exchange them for better.

Thus far the post kitchens and mess rooms and company cooks had provided three bountiful meals a day; and except for a few days on the march we scarcely made the acquaintance of the hard tack and bacon, now so affectionately remembered by men who then grumbled at the soft bread, fresh beef and vegetables so profusely furnished us at Fort Snelling.

During these busy days Regimental Headquarters were graced with the presence of Mrs. and Miss Van Cleve, the Colonel's wife and daughter, whose kindly interest in every thing that concerned the regiment was always manifest and will be always gratefully remembered by the men. At this writing (1890) both of these ladies are among the surviving and honorary members of the regiment.

CHAPTER II.

GOING TO THE WAR.

On the morning of the 14th of October, 1861, the regiment embarked on a large river steamboat under orders for Washington, D. C. An hour later we had disembarked at the upper levee in St. Paul for a parade march through the city. The people had come out in masses to see us off, and Third street from the Seven Corners to the lower levee was lined with crowds of enthusiastic men, women and children, who waved hats, handkerchiefs and flags and greeted our passing column with cheers, and smiles, and tears and blessings, that at times drowned the gay music of the band and broke up the rythmic tramp of our platoons in spite of our efforts to be, or at least to appear, soldierly.

None of us could then predict that of the thousand muskets, less than three hundred, and of the thirty-six swords, only three should at last return with the colors then so proudly floating over us. The thought was, however, in every heart that we had taken our lives in our hands to be laid down wherever and whenever duty might call for them.

The march ended at the lower levee, where we re-embarked and proceeded down the river. Throngs of loyal people greeted us at every landing, the friends of the several companies having come from their homes, some of them from interior towns, to bid the boys a last good-by.

At LaCrosse we were transferred to the railroad and arrived without noteworthy adventure at Chicago on the morning of the 16th, and were marched to and quartered in the "Wigwam," the large temporary building where Abraham Lincoln had been nominated for the presidency at the National Republican Convention the year before.

Here the company officers were ordered to keep the men strictly within the building until they should be marched out again under arms. The building was large enough not to be crowded with a thousand men, but not being intended for continuous habitation was destitute of certain conveniences, which are as necessary for soldiers as for other human beings, and most of the companies had to be marched out in the evening for exercise, etc., in the open streets, where the maneuvers greatly astonished the spectators.

We spent the night in the Wigwam and marched the next day to the Pittsburg and Fort Wayne R. R. depot, and boarded a train for Pittsburg, where we arrived in the afternoon of the 18th.

Here we were most hospitably received and marched to a public hall, where a bountiful hot supper was served by an association of loyal and generous ladies, who personally attended the tables, to which the soldiers did ample justice. This kind reception, and others like it, were not lost upon the soldiers. They remembered and talked of them wherever they went, and many a camp fire was brightened by the memory of the kind words and gracious and sympathetic attentions of loyal women, to whom all Union soldiers were as sons and brothers.

Here our orders were changed from Washington, D. C., to Kentucky, and on the 19th we embarked on three small steamers, and after a delightful voyage down the Ohio river, landed at Louisville on the 22nd.

At his invitation, the writer accompanied Col. Van Cleve to headquarters, where he reported the arrival of the regiment to Gen. W. T. Sherman, then commanding the Department of the Cumberland. This was six days after the famous conference at Louisville between General Sherman and the Secretary of War, at which the Secretary was so plainly informed that if Kentucky was to be held for the Union, troops and arms and equipage must be sent there as well as to Virginia and Missouri, and the change at Pittsburg of our destination was one of the immediate results of that conference. It was at the time a great disappointment to us, but we did not complain and soon ceased altogether to regret it.

General Sherman received us in an absent-minded sort of way, walking back and forth in his office. He asked a few disconnected questions, evidently thinking of other things as well as of us, and ended the brief interview by ordering us by rail that evening to Lebanon Junction, thirty miles distant, south, on the Louisville and Nashville R. R. We were loaded on a train of open flat cars and spent the night in a cold rain storm, making the trip at about six miles per hour, stopping a while at every side track, and occasionally where there was no siding.

About four o'clock A. M. we disembarked and stacked arms in a field near the Junction and stood around in the soft mud until sunrise, to keep ourselves awake that we might be ready to entertain any party of the enemy who might make us an early morning call.

Here we relieved the 19th Illinois regiment, then commanded by Colonel J. B. Turchin.

Sometime in the day, October 23rd, our baggage and tents arrived on another train, which had started with us, but in some inexplainable manner had actually run slower than we did. Our camp was set in regulation style, in a field just within the angle formed by the main and Lebanon branch tracks, and at "retreat," camp guard was mounted and we considered the war begun so far as we were concerned.

We remained here several weeks, sending out detachments to guard the railroad bridges in the vicinity, and keeping up the round of guard and picket duty, drill and instruction. "Reveille" was sounded an hour before daylight, and we then had to "stand to arms" until sunrise to guard against a surprise by the enemy.

The camp ground was damp and unhealthy, and in this tedious morning hour the fog settled over us like a cold wet blanket. Our sick list increased considerably until the ground was drained by deep ditches between the rows of tents, and the practice was adopted of serving every man at early "roll call" a cup of hot coffee and a hard tack, which kept him warm and cheerful until breakfast time.

Here the paymaster called upon us and squared our accounts to the 31st of October, and here we enjoyed our first Thanksgiving dinner as soldiers.

On the 15th of November, Gen. D. C. Buell assumed the command at Louisville, and on the 2nd of December organized the troops in Kentucky into the "Army of the Ohio."

Gen. Geo. H. Thomas assumed command, on the 6th, of the First Division, comprised of the First, Second and Third Brigades.

These were composed as follows:

First Brigade: Brig. Gen. Albin Schoepf, commanding.
    33rd Reg. Indiana Volunteers, Col. John Coburn.
    17th Reg. Ohio Volunteers, Col. J. M. Connell.
    12th Reg. Kentucky Volunteers, Col. W. A. Hoskins.
    38th Reg. Ohio Volunteers, Col. E. D. Bradley.

Second Brigade: Col. M. D. Manson, commanding.
    4th Reg. Kentucky Volunteers, Col. S. S. Fry.
    14th Reg. Ohio Volunteers, Col. J. B. Steedman.
    10th Reg. Indiana Volunteers, Lieut. Col. W. S. Kise.
    10th Reg. Kentucky Volunteers, Col. J. M. Harlan.

Third Brigade: Col. R. L. McCook, commanding.
    18th Reg. United States Infantry, Col. H. B. Carrington.
    2nd Reg. Minnesota Volunteers, Col. H. P. Van Cleve.
    35th Reg. Ohio Volunteers, Col. F. Van Derveer.
    9th Reg. Ohio Volunteers, Lieut. Col. G. Kammerling.

Unassigned, but later attached to First Division.
    1st Reg. Kentucky Cavalry, Col. F. Wolford.
    Battery "B" First Ohio Artillery, Capt. W. B. Standardt.
    Battery "C" First Ohio Artillery, Capt. D. Kenny.
    Battery "B" First Kentucky Artillery, Capt. Wetmore.
    A Batallion of Michigan Engineer troops, Lieut. Col. K. A. Hunton.

On the 8th of December the 3rd Minnesota regiment arrived to relieve us at Lebanon Junction, and the next day we went by rail thirty-seven miles, to Lebanon, where Gen. Thomas had established his headquarters.

Now, for the first time, we were brigaded with other troops and had the opportunity to compare our own with other regiments. The 9th Ohio, whose Colonel (Robert L. McCook) was our brigade commander, was composed entirely of Germans, few of whom could speak English. The regiment had been enlisted at Cincinnati, and had seen several months of active service, in West Virginia, participating in the engagements more or less important, at Phillippi, Rich Mountain and Carnifex Ferry. Their manual and tactics were those of the German army, as many of their officers had seen service there. Naturally, with their experience in actual war, they regarded us as comparatively fresh and we modestly respected them as veterans, intending, however, to stay with them in any controversy we might have by and by with the common enemy.

The 35th Ohio was also our senior by several months of service, mostly in Kentucky, but not having been in any battle and using our language and tactics, they did not claim nor were they conceded any superiority.

Both these regiments were brigaded with ours from this time until their muster out at the expiration of three years of service, and we had time and opportunity for close acquaintance and comradeship, which we remember pleasantly after these many years.

The 18th United States Regular Infantry was then one of the newly organized regiments of three battalions of eight companies each. They held themselves somewhat apart from us volunteers, and before we had got fairly on the same plane with them as soldiers, they were placed with other regular regiments in a brigade by themselves, the 87th Indiana taking their place in our brigade.

Here we came into the immediate presence of Geo. H. Thomas, then a new Brigadier General of Volunteers, with whom as our Division, Corps or Army commander, we served continuously for the next three years, until the beginning of the "Grand March to the Sea" in November, 1864.

Of him as a man, a soldier or a commander, no man who has ever served with him has any words except of respectful admiration.

We remained in camp at Lebanon about three weeks, devoting the time mainly to battalion drill and to general instruction in military duties. Our camp ground was reasonably fit for the purpose, the weather not unpleasant for the season, rations were fully and regularly issued, and altogether we fared better as soldiers than we knew or appreciated at the time.

Our band had well improved the long intervals at Fort Snelling and Lebanon Junction, and our parade-marches and dress parades and guard mounts, duly illustrated the "pomp and circumstance of war." Among the things, the importance of which was to be better appreciated later, was

H. P. VAN CLEVE, Colonel,
July 22, 1861, to March 22, 1862,
Brig General, U. S. V.

the coeducation of the wagoners and the mules. This was begun here and some progress made. The earlier lessons afforded a good deal of entertainment to those not engaged in them, but were sadly demoralizing to the wagoners. It has been stated that no man ever broke a team of six green army mules without breaking his christian character, if he had any, and the army chaplain who offered the long standing reward of one hundred dollars to the man who should drive such a team for thirty days without the use of profane language, did not have to part with his money.

With all the comforts of the situation here, we grew weary of mere preparation, and the announcement that we were about to commence an active campaign received a general and genuine welcome in the camp.

CHAPTER III.

THE MILL SPRINGS CAMPAIGN.

On the morning of the 1st of January, 1862, our brigade folded the tents, loaded the baggage train, and, with bands playing and colors displayed, marched out on the Columbia "pike."

Thirteen wagons were allotted for the tents and baggage of each regiment, and they were loaded to their roofs. Each man was expected to carry his rifle and accoutrements, with forty rounds of ball cartridges, knapsack with all his personal property, overcoat, blanket, canteen and haversack with three days' rations in it, a load of forty to fifty pounds.

We marched that day fourteen miles, and the next, twelve miles, encamping near Campbellsville. Here we found that most of the men were tired, sore-footed and hungry, and many of them had lost their overcoats, blankets, or some other part of their loads on the way. The roads were, however, hard and smooth, and our wagons came up in good season, so we made comfortable camps.

We remained here four days while the wagon trains went back to Lebanon and returned with more rations and supplies, and on the 7th we marched again with somewhat better preparation than before; the men carrying more rations, and less unnecessary stuff in their knapsacks, and made twelve miles comfortably.

On the 8th we passed through Columbia, and here leaving the "pike" we turned eastward on the "dirt road." It immediately began to rain, and before night the road was almost impassable. The next ten days were spent alternately in short but tedious marches in the mud and slush and rain, and in waiting for the wagon trains to come up, so about half the nights and days the troops, without shelter, were lying in the woods or fields along the roadside. This in mid-winter was a very discouraging experience to the volunteers then on their first campaign. Yet they learned speedily to make themselves as comfortable as the circumstances permitted, and things were never so bad that some fun could not be had.

General Buell had issued an order that no private property should be appropriated by the troops without proper authority, and thus far the fuel had been provided by the quartermaster, but one evening we encamped in some open fields where there was no cut wood or forest accessible. The fields were however well fenced with dry rails and, after some exasperating delay, authority was obtained to use in this emergency "only the top rail" of the fence along the color line. The cheery camp fires were soon blazing and we had plenty of fuel all the night; next morning the fence was entirely gone. The company commanders were called to account for its disappearance, but were unable to find any man who took any but the "top rail."

As we passed through the country we found usually only old men, women and children at home, most of the able bodied citizens having joined some regiment on one side or the other. In some cases brothers had enlisted in opposing regiments. Generally the people at home were not seriously foraged upon or molested, but pigs and geese occasionally did come into the camps and were duly "mustered into the army."

On the 12th of January we encamped about noon near an old time "apple jack" still. It had recently been in operation and a considerable quantity of the seductive product thereof was yet in the rude building. This was speedily appropriated by the soldiers as "contraband of war," and a night of uncommon hilarity in the camps resulted.

On the 17th of January the head of the column arrived at Logan's Crossroads, nine miles north of

Zollicoffer's intrenched camp at Beech Grove and seven miles west of Somerset, where the first brigade, commanded by General Schoepf, was posted. Beech Grove was a naturally good position on the north bank of the Cumberland, on the east side of Oak Creek at its junction with the river. Mill Springs, by which name the campaign and battle are known in our history, was on the south bank of the Cumberland opposite Beech Grove, and had no relation to the battle as far as is known; neither had Fishing Creek, from which the Confederates named the affair that took place on the 19th at Logan's Crossroads. Here we halted for the closing up of the column and to await Schoepf's brigade, which was ordered to join us.

The first and second East Tennessee (Union) infantry regiments, under Brig. General Carter, were temporarily attached to our division at this time, also a battalion of Michigan Engineer troops. On the 18th, of the forces present, the 2nd Minnesota, 9th Ohio and 12th Kentucky, with the Engineer battalion, were encamped around Thomas' headquarters on the Columbia-Somerset road, three quarters of a mile west of Logan's house. At and near Logan's house were the 4th Kentucky, 10th Indiana and the 1st and 2nd East Tennessee, the battalion of Wolford's Cavalry and two Ohio batteries, Kenny's and Standart's; Schoepf with Wetmore's Kentucky battery, the 33rd Indiana and 17th and 38th Ohio, were at Somerset; and the 10th Kentucky and 14th Ohio were on the road some miles back towards Columbia; all these forces joined us the afternoon or evening after the battle, as did the 35th Ohio. The 18th regulars were still further away and did not arrive till several days afterwards. So we had present and available for the battle seven regiments, two battalions and two batteries. Only four regiments and the battalion of cavalry were, however, engaged seriously enough to have any casualties.

General Crittenden, the confederate commander, in his report gives his order of march, naming in his column of attack eight regiments, three battalions and two batteries. All his regiments were engaged in the battle and lost heavily on the field, according to his official report and casualty list.

From a point midway between Thomas' headquarters and Logan's farm, where the Columbia-Somerset road runs nearly east and west, a road led in a southwesterly direction to the Cumberland river, passing about half a mile south of headquarters, and is called the Jamestown road. Another road led from Logan's farm southward to Beech Grove and Mill Springs, and is called the Mill Springs road in the reports. The battlefield of the 19th was on both sides of this road, and from half a mile to a mile south from the crossroads or junction at Logan's house. The ground was undulating and mostly covered with thick woods and brush, with some small open fields enclosed by the usual rail fences of the country.

About five o'clock in the afternoon of the 18th, Company "A" went out on the Jamestown road and assumed the "Grand guard" duty, posting our reserve about half a mile south of our camp, with an advance post eighty rods further out and with a line of pickets thence extending to the right and to the left and connecting in the last direction with those of the East Tennessee, and they with those of the 10th Indiana, which in a similar manner guarded the Mill Springs road, their reserve post being perhaps a mile east of ours across the fields.

We had hardly got into place when darkness and rain were upon us; the darkest night and the coldest and most pitiless and persistent rain we ever knew. It was with great difficulty that the pickets could be visited or relieved at all during the night, and the cooking of supper or even of coffee was, in the absence of shelter, out of the question. Nothing happened to break the tedious monotony of the night, but it has often since occurred to us, that if we had known that Crittenden's forces had at midnight turned out of their comfortable tents and dry blankets and for the next six weary hours were sloshing along in the mud and storm and darkness, we could have much enjoyed the contemplation of their physical and spiritual condition. It was always some comfort to the soldier on such a night as this, to think that his enemy over there, was at least as wet and cold and wretched as he was himself.

Just at daybreak arms were taken and preparations were being made to relieve the pickets, when a musket shot, another, and then five or six more in quick succession rang out with startling distinctness over on the Mill Springs road, a mile or more to our left and front. This was the first rebel shot we had ever heard. At last the enemy! now we were going to have a battle. Our first thought was, "they are making a feint on that road while they come in force on ours," which was the widest and best traveled one. Every man was keenly awake and alive with expectation, when again on the Mill Springs road the firing broke out, nearer than before, scattering at first, then thicker and faster as the enemy's advance struck the picket reserve. After a few minutes all was still again at the front, but in the camps behind us the long-roll was beating and the companies were forming in hot haste, and presently we heard our regiment and the 9th Ohio moving off towards Logan's farm.

Then the firing broke out again as the enemy came up to the 10th Indiana and later on to the 4th Kentucky, those regiments having hastily got into position in the woods about half a mile in front of their camp. Here the enemy were held for some time and were compelled to bring up and deploy their two brigades for an attack in full force. In the meantime the 2nd Minnesota and 9th Ohio arrived, (nine companies of each,) and in good order were put into the fight under General Thomas' personal direction, the 2nd taking the line first occupied successively by the 10th and 4th, which regiments were retired to replenish their ammunition, and the 9th Ohio forming on its right; the Mill Springs road dividing the two newly arrived regiments.

The new line was immediately advanced some distance through the woods, guiding on the road. The rain had now ceased but the air was loaded with mist and smoke, and the underbrush in our part of the field was so thick that a man was hardly visible a musket's length away. Suddenly the 2nd's line came against a rail fence with an open field in front and a line of the enemy's troops were dimly seen through the mist some twenty or thirty rods distant in the field. The firing commenced immediately and in a few minutes the enemy's line, just mentioned, had disappeared. It was in fact his second line, the first being literally under the guns and noses of the 2nd regiment, only the fence intervening. The sudden arrival of the 2nd at this fence was a surprise to the rebel 20th Tennessee, which was already just arrived there, and it was a surprise also to our boys to discover, in the heat of the engagement, that the opposite side of the fence was lined with recumbent rebels. Here, as Col. R. L. McCook says in his official report, "the contest was at first almost hand-to-hand; the enemy and the 2nd Minnesota were poking their guns through the same fence." This condition of things could not and did not last long after our boys really discovered and got after them; many of the enemy were killed and wounded there, but more after they got up and were trying to get away. Some remained and surrendered. One lieutenant, as the firing ceased and the smoke lifted, stood a few feet in front of Company "I" of the 2nd and calmly faced his fate. His men had disappeared and he was called on to surrender. He made no reply but raising his revolver fired into our ranks with deliberate aim, shooting Lieut. Stout through the body. Further parley was useless and he was shot dead where he stood. He was young Bailie Peyton, the son of a noble sire, whose sword, presented by the citizens of New Orleans for his gallant service in the Mexican war, was here found on the dead body of his son. We met his father later at his home near Gallatin, Tennessee. He was one of the foremost Union men of his state and it was an inexpressible grief to him that his only son should have enlisted in the Rebel cause. He said that his only comfort was, in the reflection that he did not die as a coward.

The enemy in front of the 9th Ohio, sheltered by some buildings and fences, obstinately maintained their position and a bayonet charge, in which part of the 2nd joined, was finally ordered and made and this finished the fight.

In the meantime, at our post on the Jamestown road, we listened to the battle in a state of excitement which I cannot attempt to describe.

As the regiments moved out of camp towards the field, and the heavier volleys seemed to settle the question that it was to be a battle over there and not a feint, we (of Company A) had about decided to abandon our post and join the regiment, when the Lieut. Colonel commanding the Engineer battalion rode up and said General Thomas had left him in charge of all guards and picket details, and ordered us to stack arms and remain where we were. His battalion came out a few minutes later and halted near us. We begged him to relieve us, but entreaty or argument availed nothing with him until the final conflict, just described, had fairly opened with a volley of musketry more terrible than before, and so long continued as to leave no possible doubt. Then he conceded that we were no longer needed at our post, and consented that we should go to the field with the reserve only, leaving all the men out on the picket line and advance post. So we started on a run across the plowed fields in a direct line for the battle. As we approached the woods we were obliged to deflect somewhat to the left to find an open way, and finally got into the Mill Springs road about a quarter of a mile north of the battle-ground, just as the final charge was made. The yelling of the charging regiments was, if possible, more stimulating to us than the musketry had been, but, in fact, we were nearly exhausted physically when we turned southward in the narrow winding road towards the field of battle. Now we met the stragglers and skulkers and the wounded. On the first stretcher was the body of Lieut Stout, and one of the bearers was that courtly gentleman and honored citizen, Mr. Charles Scheffer, of St. Paul. He was then State Treasurer, and had on the previous day taken from our regiment the allotments of pay then authorized to be paid to families or dependents at home. He had gone out to the battle with the regiment and had found this opportunity to render kind service to the wounded men. As we approached the fighting ground the trees were flecked with bullets and the underbrush had been cut away as with a scythe, the dead and wounded lay along the fence, on one the blue, on the other the gray; further on the enemy's dead were everywhere scattered across the open field, and lay in a windrow along the ridge where the second line had stood. We halted a moment where the body of General Zollicoffer lay beside the wagon track. He had been shot through the heart by Colonel Fry, of the 4th Kentucky, early in the battle. The two officers, each with an aid, had met in the narrow winding roadway as they were respectively getting their troops into position in the woods on each side of it. All wore waterproof coats or ponchos, and at first did not recognize each other as enemies. As soon as they did, revolvers were drawn; Zollicoffer's aid fired at Col. Fry and got out of the way, leaving his chief to fall by the return he had invited. The body had been dragged out of the way of passing artillery and wagons, and lay by the fence, the face upturned to the sky and bespattered with mud from the feet of marching men and horses. It was decently cared for later, and, with that of Lieut. Bailie Peyton, was sent through the lines to Nashville for interment. We soon found our regiment and joined it. The battle was over, and the mob of demoralized fugitives in the distance were rapidly getting out of sight.

Col. Van Cleve sent a messenger to relieve and bring up our men left on the picket line, and, as the advance was being resumed, gave us the lead. The pursuit was, however, tedious and uneventful. Occasionally a few shots were exchanged with the enemy's rear guard, and some exhausted or wounded stragglers captured were all we had to enliven the chase until we approached Moulden's hill, a high ridge within a mile of and commanding the intrenched camp at Beech Grove. Here a show of resistance was made, and General Thomas halted and developed his forces in order of attack. The advance up the easy slope of the hill was an inspiring spectacle to us, but the enemy did not remain to enjoy it. When our skirmish line reached the crest of the ridge their rear guard was seen in full retreat again, and soon disappeared within their camp. Our batteries were brought up, and one of them, posted on the left near the river, practised a while with shell on a little steamer crossing and recrossing the stream at a point below the camp, provoking a reply from the enemy's guns which, however, did us no harm.

The sun was yet an hour high and, as it afterwards appeared, an immediate advance upon the camp would have met with no formidable organized resistance, though it was well protected by breastworks, abbattis and entanglements. Some valuable lives would, however, have been lost in an assault at that time, and probably most of the enemy would have escaped, as they afterwards did, by dispersion, but without immediately crossing the river. The truth, not then known, but generally suspected, was that the demoralized rebels were crossing the Cumberland as fast as they could, and most of the men got over before morning.

After a brief survey of the situation as far as it was then to be seen, General Thomas bivouacked his troops in line of battle where they were first halted; and during the evening the other regiments of his command which had not been in the battle, came up, except the 18th regulars. The night was clear and cold, and the men of Company "A" had had no food or rest during the thirty hours past, and none of the regiments had eaten during the day. The exposure to the storm during the night, the excitement and physical exhaustion of the morning's wild race across the soft ploughed field, of the battle and the day's tramp, began to tell.

Rations had been spoiled in the haversacks by the rain, or left behind in the morning, and not until nine or ten o'clock in the evening, when the trains came up, was anything procurable to eat.

That night's exposure broke down many strong men in our regiment who never recovered for duty.

Next morning our regiment marched into the camp of the 20th Tennessee, within the intrenchments, and filed off into the company streets just as we would have done in our own. Apparently the 20th men had not visited their tents at all since they had left them at midnight to attack us; provisions, clothing, blankets and all the comforts that accumulate about a soldier during a month in camp, were here in profusion. All the camps were left by the enemy's regiments in like manner, the tents standing and officers' baggage and personal effects, and supplies of all sorts, in hospitable abandonment. All the artillery, except one gun left back mired in the mud, was found fully horsed and standing in the narrow roadway leading down into the valley from the camp; the leading gun had locked a wheel on a small tree, and the whole train had been then and there abandoned; more than a thousand horses and mules were frolicking about the valley, helping themselves to forage from the unguarded piles. A few wagons hastily loaded with baggage were found on the steamboat landing, awaiting a crossing that was not to be made. A few sick, wounded and skulkers were added to our list of prisoners, but the army that had a few hours before marched out in that midnight storm to surprise "old Pap Thomas," was now scattered all over the country south of the Cumberland, every man getting away as fast and as far as he could. Probably not many of those men were ever brought together again as organized regiments; they certainly spread dismay and consternation all over the country wherever they went, and probably thus contributed much to succeeding Union victories in Tennessee.

The little steamer, which had been for twelve hours so busily engaged in crossing the stampeded rebels, was set on fire by the last to cross, and drifted down the river and out of sight.

Schoepf's brigade was sent on the 21st across the river to pursue the enemy, but there was no enemy to pursue and he returned. On the same day we returned to our camp at Logan's crossroads, and the 22nd was spent in issuing supplies. The dead of both armies were buried on the 20th and 21st, and the wounded were cared for as well as the circumstances permitted.

On the 23rd we marched to Somerset, and thence southward about two miles. Our trains were mired in the road near Fishing Creek, about three miles from Logan's, and we spent a miserable night without shelter. On the 24th we encamped in a pleasant field on the north bank of the Cumberland river, where we made ourselves comfortable for a few days. Meantime our sick and wounded men were distributed in all the available buildings in and near Somerset, and in these temporary hospitals were cared for as well as could be under the circumstances. Many a brave fellow who, in anticipation of a battle had cheerfully endured the hardships of the march, now succumbed. The sick largely outnumbered the wounded, and our permanent loss from disease originating or developed in this campaign was more than 15 per cent. of the total force, while the killed and wounded was less than 7½ per cent. of the troops engaged, and many of the wounded were only temporarily disabled. Of the campaign it might be said that the march would have been a severe one even for veterans.

The battle was on both sides desperately contested while it lasted, but was soon over, and the victory on the field was decisive and complete.

Among the trophies was a flag of the Fifteenth Mississippi, captured by the Second Minnesota, and by General Thomas forwarded to the war department. (*Appendix No. 8.*)

This flag is among those now awaiting the direction of Congress and, let it be hoped, of the Grand Army of the Republic, as to their final disposition.

Another trophy that now reposes in the goodly company of war worn flags, in the Adjutant General's office at the capitol of Minnesota, is a handsome banner with the inscription: "Mill Springs, "Jan'y 19, 1862, 2nd Reg't Minn. Vol. Inf'y.

"Presented in behalf of the Loyal Ladies of Louisville, "Ky." This was in commemoration of this battle and victory; which redeemed Kentucky to the Union of States, not to be seriously or permanently occupied by the Confederates again during the war.

The casualties of the nine companies engaged of our regiment were 12 killed and 33 wounded. In the four regiments (and Wolford's battalion) engaged, the Union loss was 40 killed and 207 wounded. Total casualties 247. The Confederate loss was stated by General Crittenden at 126 killed, 309 wounded and 99 missing, total 534; but General Thomas reports the Confederate dead, buried by our troops, at 192 and the unwounded prisoners at 89, which with the 309 wounded and 10 missing, not captured, would make the Confederate loss 600; under the circumstances Thomas must be conceded to be the better authority as to the dead and prisoners. On the other hand, Crittenden, who could have had no knowledge of the Union loss, estimates it at 700, and says "It was "larger than mine from the fact that my regiments "on the left after having been first driven back fired "from the cover of woods and fences upon a large "number advancing upon them through an open "field, inflicting heavy loss and sustaining but little."

He had, in fact, more than twice as many men engaged as we did, and his loss on the field was to ours about in the same proportion; so if it were or were not true that his troops were the better sheltered the fire of our men must have been the better directed and delivered. (*Appendix Nos. 9, 10, 11 and 12.*)

CHAPTER IV.

MILL SPRINGS TO SHILOH.

On the 10th of February, we folded our tents again and began the return march to Louisville. In the afternoon we camped a mile north of Somerset, where we remained the next day and said "good-by" to many of our comrades in the hospitals who were too sick or too badly wounded to be moved. Here it rained and snowed alternately, as it did in fact, nearly every day of the march to the Ohio river. The roads were almost impassable and the companies were ordered each to march with its wagon to help it along as it often became necessary to do.

On the 14th we arrived at Crab Orchard where we struck the "pike," as macadamized roads are always called in that country, and thenceforward the march was less tedious, though the weather did not much improve.

On the 15th we passed through Stanford and on the 16th arrived at Danville where we rested one day while it rained.

On the 18th made a long march, passing through Perryville, halting there only long enough to observe the academy with its garrison of bright-eyed school-girls, and encamped within two or three miles of Lebanon.

On the 19th we marched all day in a drenching rain-storm and encamped on the farm of Dr. Jackson, a brother of the man who killed Col. Ellsworth at

Alexandria, Va., in the summer of 1861. The doctor was absent under military arrest, but his hospitality was freely drawn upon by the tired, wet and hungry soldiers, who left nothing there next morning that could be drunk, eaten or carried away.

On the 24th we passed through Bardstown and on the 25th arrived at Louisville about 3 P. M., and were received with most enthusiastic welcome. The sidewalks were full of loyal men and flags were waved to us from windows and porches as we gaily marched the principal streets towards the river. At the National Hotel the regiment was halted and faced to the front while a deputation of the "Loyal Ladies of Louisville," came out and presented the beautiful silk banner referred to in a preceding chapter. After a brief response by Col. Van Cleve our march was resumed and we went on board the large steamer "Jacob Strader" at the levee.

Meantime on the 6th, Fort Henry, and on the 16th, Fort Donelson, had been captured and the way was now open to Nashville by the Ohio and Cumberland rivers.

On the 26th our baggage, mules and wagons were taken aboard at Portland, just below the falls and three miles from Louisville levee, and we proceeded down the river, very glad of the change from marching to sailing.

On the 28th we arrived at Smithfield, where we entered the Cumberland and passed Fort Donelson on the 1st of March and Clarksville on the 2nd, arriving at Nashville next day. On the 4th we disembarked and encamped about three miles out of the city on the "Granny White Pike." Here we had a pleasant and healthy camp and fine spring weather. Ample supplies of clothing, rations and ammunition were issued and accumulated, and a good many of our sick and slightly wounded, who had been left behind, now joined us for duty.

Meantime arrangements had been made for a junction of Buell's and Halleck's forces to be made near the great bend of the Tennessee river; Savannah, on the right bank, being finally designated by Gen. Halleck as the point.

On the 16th of March, McCook's division of Buell's army commenced the march towards the appointed rendezvous, followed in order, one day apart, by those of Nelson, Crittenden, Wood and Thomas. Our division (Thomas') having had a battle already, was in this new campaign assigned to the rear of the column, and marched on the 20th, passing through the city and out on the Franklin pike some eight or ten miles. On the 21st we passed through Franklin and camped a few miles south of the village, remaining there the 22nd. On the 23rd we moved up two or three miles to Spring Hill, and here we found the road ahead of us occupied by the camps and trains of the preceding divisions.

The bridge over Duck River at Columbia had been destroyed. The river was at flood height, no pontoons or other bridge material was available, and we all waited six days for the water to subside.

On the 29th a bridge was improvised, and a ford, deep and rapid, but practicable with care, was found, and the crossing was commenced. It was slow and tedious work, and it was not until the 2nd of April that ours, the rear division, had a clear way to proceed. On the 4th the road ahead of us was so obstructed with the trains of the other divisions that we remained in camp; it was raining heavily all day and night.

On this day General Grant telegraphed in reply to Nelson's message of the 3rd that he could be at Savannah with his division on the 5th, that he (Nelson) need not hasten his march, as transports to convey him to Pittsburg Landing would not be ready before the 8th. (*Van Horne's History, Army of Cumberland, Vol. 1, page 103.*)

The rain ceased on the 5th, and we marched about twelve miles, keeping close up to the column leading us. Next day, the 6th, the troops ahead of us seemed to be showing more speed, and we began to pass the wagon trains as we overtook them, instead of keeping behind them as we had been doing; so, notwithstanding the bad condition of the roads and frequent detours to pass around the stalled wagon trains, we marched twenty-two miles before dark. During the afternoon, whenever we halted to rest, we could hear the rumbling of the cannonade in the distant west, and we knew that a great battle was in progress. About sunset it commenced to rain again, and speedily grew so dark that a man in the column could scarcely see his file leader within arm's reach. Still we tramped on, tired, cold, wet and hungry, until about eleven o'clock, when our brigade was turned into a soft plowed cotton field, to spend the rest of the night.

The situation here would have been utterly forlorn had it not been enlivened by the order at midnight to "cook three days' rations and be ready to march at 4 o'clock A. M." As it rained all night, the fence rails were laid in the mud for bedding or "standing room"; no other fuel was available, and the rations were in the wagons, miles behind us. So the cooking was omitted, but we were ready and glad to march at daybreak.

The halts on the 7th were few and short, but our progress, in the wretched condition of the road, was slow and tedious, though we marched towards the sound of the guns all day. We arrived at Savannah in the afternoon of the 8th, to spend another night in the rain without shelter, but had time before dark to select a grass field for our bivouac and get rails and other firewood to cook and sleep by. Here we heard that the field of Shiloh had been won and was held by our Union forces, so we rested contentedly. Next morning, April 9th, steamers came to Savannah for us, and embarking, we were taken up to Pittsburg Landing, and at noon stacked arms and rested on the battle field. The weather had cleared up, and though our wagons and tents did not arrive for several days, we were comfortable enough without them. The burial of the dead and collection of the wounded now fully occupied a large portion of our men for two or three days.

The official reports state the Union loss at 1,754 killed, 8,408 wounded and 2,885 captured or missing; and the Confederate loss at 1,728 killed, 8,012 wounded and 959 missing. Of the missing many were undoubtedly killed or wounded; so we had to perform the burial of about 4,000 men, gathering them from every part of the battle field. Some lay where they had first fallen, others lived long enough to crawl to some near-by thicket or gully, for protection or for water; some lay in attitudes of rest, their faces showing nothing of suffering or fear, others had evidently died in great agony. Some were identified by comrades, and of such the graves were rudely marked; but many of our dead and nearly all the Confederates were unknown and unrecognized. They were laid side by side in long shallow pits and were covered, a hundred or more, in one grave. Many of the wounded had been able to find their own way to the field hospitals, but several thousand of them were taken up on the field and carried off on stretchers or in ambulances. Some of these were not found until two or three days after the battle.

All of this was very sad business; none who participated in it or witnessed it, will ever forget it.

Men can, in the enthusiasm and excitement of battle, see and take part in the murderous work without realizing how horrible it is, but to go over the field the day afterwards, and in cool blood to gather up the mangled and suffering victims, gives one a life-long impression of the cruelty of war and of its pitiful waste of human life.

After two or three days of this we moved out from the battle field towards Corinth five or six miles, and when our trains arrived established ourselves in camp again, in a pleasant gravelly field with shade and spring water.

Here Col. Van Cleve was promoted to Brigadier General and mustered out of the regiment, Lieut. Col. George was promoted to Colonel, Maj. Wilkin to Lieutenant Colonel and Capt. Bishop to Major; all their commissions dated March 21st, 1862.

Gen. Thomas having been assigned to command a corps of several divisions, Brig. Gen. T. W. Sherman assumed command *vice* Thomas of our division, and Lieut. Col. Wilkin was detailed as Inspector General at his headquarters. He was on detached service thereafter most of the time until he was mustered out of the regiment August 26th, 1862, to become Colonel of the 9th Minnesota volunteers.

At this camp our band was mustered out on the 24th of April, by order of Gen. Buell, and the men went home leaving most of their instruments there in the woods. The band had been an agreeable and much appreciated institution in our permanent camps, but in the hard marches of a long campaign the members got scattered and lost, and of late we had had but little music from them. They were good musicians, but did not take kindly to actual soldiering, and were no doubt quite willing to quit there.

Gen. Halleck arrived at Shiloh on the 11th of April, and after reorganizing the two armies of Buell and Grant and reinforcing them by the army of the Mississippi, under Pope, and by a division from Missouri and one from Arkansas, commenced the "seige of Corinth." A general advance and intrenchment of the Union lines about once a week, with almost daily skirmishing during the intervals, brought us at the end of May into such position that Corinth had to be defended or evacuated. A volley of explosions and a dense cloud of smoke in our front at daybreak on the 30th announced the final departure of the Confederate army, which with persistence and impudence to be admired had held our greatly superior force at bay for nearly two months. Our lines were immediately advanced, but in places met with vigorous resistance from the enemy's picket line, which had been left in position. These men were mostly captured and were immensely disgusted to learn that they had been abandoned to such a fate. This narrative is not the place to criticize general operations of armies, but it may truthfully and properly be said, that we marched into the vacated and desolate streets of Corinth that day with a feeling of disgust and humiliation at the escape of the enemy that we ought to have captured, or at least have broken up and defeated.

A show of pursuit had to be made, and we marched on after the retreating enemy for several days, passing through Danville and Rienzi. On the 6th our regiment "corduroyed" about four miles of swampy road, by transferring the rail fences from both sides to the centre of the track, where they were speedily sunk out of sight by the artillery and heavily loaded supply wagons.

On the 8th we halted at Boonville, Miss., where we remained three days. Returning we reached our old camp near Corinth on the 13th, having been out 14 days without tents or baggage, and so far as we could see had accomplished nothing.

Next day we moved three miles east from Corinth, where we got several days rest, on fresh clean ground. Some reorganization had been going on, however, in our absence, and we found Gen. Thomas in command again of our division, and preparations were soon completed for a new campaign.

CHAPTER V.

CORINTH TO LOUISVILLE.

Buell's army had been projected eastward, with Chattanooga and East Tennessee as the apparent objectives, and the divisions of McCook, Crittenden and Nelson were already well advanced in that direction, when, on the 22nd of June, our brigade broke camp and commenced the march along the Memphis and Charleston railroad, repairing it as we went along, reaching Iuka Springs on the 25th. The other two brigades of our division were several days' march in advance of us, and, as we moved eastward, troops from Grant's army followed, and were stationed in detachments to guard the railroad bridges left behind us.

At Iuka we were paid off for two months, chiefly in the then new postal currency, which we had not before seen. Col. George here left us on "sick leave."

On the 27th our march eastward was resumed, and our regiment arrived on the 29th at Tuscumbia, Ala. We encamped in an open field, just at the edge of the village, and near a remarkably copious spring of pure water. Here Gen. Thomas' division was assembled again, and on the 4th of July we had a national salute from the three batteries and a grand parade of twelve regiments, after which some appropriate and patriotic addresses were made by Gov. Alex. Ramsey, of Minnesota, Gens. Steedman and McCook, and perhaps others.

Gov. Ramsey's visit at this time and place, though brief, gave him opportunity to see and compare the 2nd Minnesota regiment with those from other states, and he was, as he said, quite satisfied with our representation of the state.

Finding ourselves located here for some considerable time, our camp was put in good order and made comfortable, and the usual course of company and battalion drill and instruction was instituted. The "company musicians," who in presence of the "band" had been quite overlooked, if not forgotten, were now hunted up and investigated. Those who were not in fact *musicians* were exchanged in their companies for other men who were, or could become such; a "principal musician" was appointed, bugles and fifes and drums were supplied to them, and the same discipline applied to them that prevailed with the other men of the regiment. A few weeks of faithful instruction and practice made them quite proficient in martial music, and the "bugle band" of the 2nd Minnesota received a good deal of attention and commendation from the other regiments, and was much appreciated by our own men.

On the 26th of July our pleasant camp here was broken up, and we crossed the Tennessee river to Florence. We were told that Gen. Andrew Jackson had crossed the river here just fifty years before, on his way to New Orleans, in 1812. The next day being Sunday, the usual inspection of troops was had, and this over, a good many officers and enlisted men of the several regiments availed themselves of the opportunity to attend divine service. The Presbyterian church was well filled, the usual congregation of resident women and children occupying perhaps one third of the seats. The uniformed visitors were courteously received and ushered in, mingling with the regular attendants wherever there might be room. The opening services were of the usual character, and the singing was heartily joined in by the soldiers; the scripture readings were attentively listened to, and all heads were reverently bowed when the venerable minister said "let us pray." The prayer, we were afterwards told, was the formal one prescribed by the Presbyterian church authority of the South, and contained an invocation of the divine blessing upon the "President of the Confederate States and "upon all in authority under him," and upon the armies of the Confederate States, and a direct and earnest appeal that confusion and defeat might overwhelm their enemies, who had invaded their soil and threatened their institutions and their liberties. This had not been generally expected by the visitors, and it produced at the instant quite an appreciable commotion. A variety of ejaculations, not in the usual line of liturgical responses, were heard in various parts of the house, and some got up and walked out to vent their indignation in the open air. Most of us remained, however, to see the services through. The prayer ended, the sermon began; a simple, earnest, well composed and well delivered discourse, interesting, edifying and every way unexceptional. The preacher was himself the personification of christian grace and dignity in the pulpit, and we were soon in the mood to ignore, if we could not forgive or forget, the offensive prayer. He had probably half completed his discourse when the tramp of marching men was heard coming down the main aisle, and a squad of the provost guard "halted" and "fronted" at the altar before the minister. A colonel of infantry led the detachment, and now he interrupted the preacher, charged him with insulting the uniform of the United States and those who wore it, in addressing a disloyal petition to the Almighty in their presence, and commanded him to come down and surrender to arrest. The minister gracefully bowed in compliance, and, closing his sermon book, came down and said he was "at your service, sir." Now the ladies interposed, some with tears and pleadings, and some with sneers and taunts at the imposing show of armed men in a peaceful church where only women and children were present to protest, and some fainted, while the colonel marched his guard and prisoner out and to headquarters. The women then appealed to those of us who remained. They were assured that their pastor was not led out to be shot, and that probably no physical harm would be done to him, and as soon as we could without rudeness, we withdrew to discuss in our camp the experiences and events of the morning. The propriety of the arrest, under the circumstances, was then hotly debated among those who were present, and the discussion has been renewed at every opportunity since. It still remains as one of the questions left unsettled at the close of the war. The prisoner was sent North under arrest, but what charges were formally preferred, or what, if any, trial or punishment he may have had, was never known to us.

On Tuesday, the 29th of July, we marched again eastward; the weather was hot and the road dusty, but there seemed to be no urgent haste, and our progress was leisurely and comfortable. The great fields, erewhile in cotton, were now all in corn, and afforded plenty of roasting ears for the soldiers and forage for the mules. The darkies came in troops from every plantation as we passed, and joined the "Lincum Sogers," bringing horses, mules, cattle, pigs, poultry, bedding and everything else they could carry. They had apparently just begun to realize what the war meant to them, and were quite ready to improve the opportunity of going out from bondage, and of despoiling their old masters as they went.

As we approached Athens we got a mail from the North, and in it some one received a copy of the song, then just published, entitled, "Kingdom Comin'." Adjt. S. P. Jennison sang it in camp that evening in his unctious and inimitable style, while the men of the regiment joined in as they learned the chorus, and a crowd of black faces grinning with delight surrounded them, taking in the spirit of the words and music, so appropriate to the situation at the time. In a day or two everybody knew and was singing it, and the darkies would have a circus over it every evening, keeping the song going with original and grotesque variations until they were suppressed by the camp guard at "taps."

On the 3rd of August we marched through Athens, Tenn. This was a lovely village, and had been noted for being the last place in the state to haul down the Union flag. The inhabitants, however, had been disgracefully plundered by Turchin's brigade of Union soldiers a short time before our arrival, and they regarded our approach with some apprehension, probably; for which they were to be excused. They were not in any way molested or inconvenienced by our presence, except from the desertion of those servants who had not already left them.

On Monday, the 5th, our brigade commander, Gen. Robert L. McCook, was murdered by a gang of guerillas. He was sick when he left Tuscumbia, and during the whole march was unable to sit up or be dressed. He had a bed made in an ambulance, in which it was his custom to ride far enough in advance of the troops to avoid the dust which always enveloped the marching column. On this day the road was narrow and sinuous, with a thick growth of small trees on each side. His ambulance, attended by two or three staff officers, was perhaps half a mile ahead of the column, in which the 35th

Ohio was the leading regiment. Suddenly a party of horsemen appeared in the road before him, and the ambulance was immediately turned and started back on the run. The party pursued with yells and firing of revolvers, and, riding up on each side, shot him through the body. The horses were frightened and beyond the control of the driver, who said the General had ordered him to stop before the fatal shot was fired. The team was forced into the thicket and the staff officers, Capts. Brooke and Miller, were captured and hurried away. The head of the column soon arrived, and the General was taken to the nearest house, while the brigade encamped around him. We had no cavalry, and the guerillas could not be overtaken. The men of the 9th Ohio (McCook's own regiment) were wild with rage, and in revenge burned every building in the neighborhood, presuming that the murderers were residents of the vicinity, as they probably were.

The General died next day and the march was at once resumed. Col. Ferdinand Van Derveer assumed command of the brigade, which he very ably administered until the expiration of his term of service, about two years later.

On the 7th of August we arrived at Winchester, Tenn., where we remained twelve days.

About this time Company "C," of the 3rd Minnesota regiment, commanded by Capt. Mills, was attached to the 2nd regiment. This company was on detached duty when its regiment was surrendered at Murfreesboro, July 13, 1862, and pending the exchange and return of their comrades was sent to us for duty. It was a fine company of soldiers, and remained with us several weeks, leaving us at Louisville on the 30th of September, for Minnesota.

On the 19th of August we moved from Winchester to Decherd, and thence by short marches and intermediate halts of one to three days to Pelham Gap, thus consuming the time to August 31st, while Bragg's army were making their way across the mountains and around our left flank towards Nashville.

During these days we got news of the Indian outbreak and massacre in Minnesota, which created much apprehension and excitement, as many of our men had families and friends in the threatened frontier counties. Lieut. Col. Alex. Wilkin was on the 26th of August appointed Colonel of the 9th Minnesota regiment, and Maj. J. W. Bishop was commissioned Lieutenant Colonel, and Capt. J. B. Davis, of Company "F," Major of the 2nd Minnesota from the same date. Adjt. S. P. Jennison, about the same time, was appointed Lieutenant Colonel of the 10th Minnesota regiment, and Lieut. Charles F. Meyer took the vacated place as Adjutant of the 2nd.

On the 1st of September we marched to Manchester, and our wagon trains with tents and baggage having been sent via Murfreesboro to Nashville, we encamped for the night in the fair-ground buildings. Next day resumed the march towards Murfreesboro, arriving there on the 4th. On the 3rd we encamped early in the day and sent details into a large melon field near by, who captured several hundred large, fine, luscious watermelons which, after our hot and dusty march, were much relished.

Pursuing our northward march we arrived at Nashville on the 7th and encamped in the edge of the city. Most of our army had already crossed the Cumberland, but it was given out that our brigade should remain at Nashville, and we did for a week, while our divisions north of the river were watching Bragg's movements. By the 14th his army was all across the Cumberland, at points higher up the river and further north than Nashville, and the race for Louisville began. Our brigade left Nashville on the 14th and crossing the river encamped just north of Edgefield. We had received five days rations of flour, coffee and sugar only, no clothing or shoes, which were especially needed. In the next three days we marched on the hard, dusty pike seventy miles to Bowling Green. Here, on the 18th, more rations of flour were issued, and we crossed the Barren river, in which we found the first supply of drinkable water since leaving the Cumberland. On the 19th we marched twenty-five miles, and on the 20th overtook our other divisions, and passing through their camps, came up to the enemy's rear picket line near Cave City. Here we extended our line of battle to right and left, and posted our picket line confronting theirs. This was the seventh day of the march which was without a parallel in our experience thus far. It was the dry season of the year, and in this part of Kentucky there was no living water, except the Barren river, between the Green and

Cumberland rivers. The farmers had depended for a scanty supply on the "sink-holes," which were saucer-like depressions in the fields, with clay sub-soil bottoms, which filled with water in winter and spring, but at this season were nearly exhausted by evaporation. Then Bragg's army was ahead of us, and they made it their business to enrich the already viscid water with dead mules and camp offal of all sorts, so it could not be drunk and could hardly be used even to mix our "dough gods." These were made by moistening our flour on a rock with water, and after pounding it into a tough dough, it was spun into a long roll, about an inch in diameter, and wound spirally around a ramrod and so baked at the camp fire. These, with scanty rations of bacon, constituted a decidedly thin diet for the hard service required of us. We had no tents or cooking utensils or baggage of any sort except such as were carried on pack mules or on the men's backs, and even these had become sadly deficient, as we had not been able to get any supplies at Nashville. Occasionally we got apples or peaches along the road, but generally the trees were cleaned by the troops ahead of us.

On this occasion, however, we found in our immediate front a big apple orchard, the trees all loaded with juicy fruit. The enemy's picket line was along the fence, on the further side, and their camps not far beyond. Our picket line was established along the fence on our side of the orchard, which was perhaps eighty rods across. Our men began to get over the fence and gather the apples, and the enemy's pickets fired at them; our pickets in turn would not let the thirsty rebels get any apples out of their side of the orchard. The situation speedily became known in the camps, and our picket line was in a few minutes reinforced by several hundred of the boys, who "straggled" out there with their guns, and presently our line was advanced with a rush to the further side of the orchard. The enemy's pickets resisted actively, but retired just before our line reached them. They made an effort to regain their fence, but our boys wouldn't give it up. The advance troops in both armies got under arms upon hearing the racket, but the affair was probably reported to the generals as a "picket skirmish" of no consequence, and all became quiet again, and our boys had the run of the orchard that night. Several of the men were wounded, but none killed, in the skirmish, which was entirely an affair of the enlisted men. It looked at one time, however, as though a general fight might grow out of it right there and then, and we were all more than willing to have it so.

This evening we got orders to cook three days' rations and prepare for a battle which would probably take place on the next day.

The enemy, however, moved on early next morning, and the foot race began again. Our division remained in camp while the others passed on and took the road ahead of us. On the 22nd we moved camp about two miles to a place near Cave City, where, at the bottom of a natural rocky pit, about a hundred feet deep, an underground stream of pure water came to the light,

A steep path and steps led down to it, and all day it was alive with soldiers, each laden with as many canteens as he could carry. The boys spent the day mainly in filling up like camels with that water, in preparation for resuming the march.

On the 23rd we started again, crossing Green river about noon, and camped on Bacon's Creek after a march of twenty miles. On the 24th we started at daybreak and marched fast all day, making thirty miles, and halted for the night four or five miles north of Elizabethtown.

The race was now telling on the footsore rebels, also, and during that and the previous day we passed their exhausted stragglers to the number of several hundred, leaving them to be gathered up as prisoners by our rear guard. Bragg's army was, however, ahead of us, and within one or two days' march of Louisville. Next day we left the railroad and parallel pike and went straight to the Ohio river, at the mouth of the Salt river, making the twenty miles in less than seven hours, and reaching the river bank about noon, a tired, hungry, ragged, foot-sore crowd. "Thank God for the Ohio river and hard tack!" exclaimed the champion grumbler of the regiment, "I'll never complain again." Here were steamers loaded with rations, clothing and shoes, and waiting to carry us to Louisville, about thirty miles up the river. With little ceremony the boxes of hard bread and bacon were rolled ashore and broken open, and, while the steamers were being loaded and departing with other troops, our brigade rested and refreshed and waited our time. Next day we embarked also, and soon after noon were at Louisville, where we found most of Buell's army encamped around and in defence of the city. The next four days were occupied in resupplying the troops with clothing, rations, ammunition and equipment, in preparation for a new and offensive campaign for the recovery and reoccupation of Kentucky and Tennessee.

During this time orders came from the war department relieving Gen. Buell, and assigning the command to Gen. Thomas; these orders were suspended by request of Gen. Thomas, and were never put into effect.

CHAPTER VI.

THE PERRYVILLE CAMPAIGN.

While in Louisville, in the last week in September, some important changes and events took place in the organization of Buell's army.

Gen. William Nelson, who had been one of the most efficient division commanders, was killed on the 29th at the Galt House, by Gen. Jefferson C. Davis, in a personal quarrel. The army was the same day reorganized into three corps; the first commanded by Gen. A. D. McCook, consisting of the divisions of Rousseau, Sill and Jackson; the second corps, commanded by Maj. Gen. Crittenden, was composed of the divisions of Wood, Van Cleve and Smith; and the third corps contained the divisions of Schoepf, Sheridan and Mitchell. To the command of this corps Gen. Buell assigned "Maj. Gen. C. C. Gilbert," by orders of September 29th. Gilbert was a Captain in the 1st United States infantry, who had been "appointed a Major General of volunteers, subject to the approval of the President," by Gen. Wright, and by him "assigned to the command of the army of Kentucky." This appointment, it appears, was never approved by the President, though a commission as Brigadier General was issued to him on the 25th of September.

Gen. Buell, supposing him to be in fact a Major General, thus placed him in command of the corps over three division commanders and two of the brigade commanders who were actually his seniors in rank. Gilbert in turn, it is said, assigned Capt. Gay of his staff to the command of the brigade of cavalry, as "Chief of Cavalry," over several colonels and field officers senior to him.

These unauthorized honors were not very modestly borne by the officers so distinguished, and within the three weeks of the following campaign, a very general protest against them was developed throughout the corps and among the men of every grade in the service. Gen. Buell was held responsible for them and so shared the censure.

Matters were getting decidedly unpleasant all around, when on the 23rd of October "Brig. Gen. C. C. Gilbert" was suddenly relieved by Gen. Buell from the command of the third corps and assigned to the tenth division, and on the next day Gen. Buell himself was, by orders from Washington, relieved from the command of the army and department, and Maj. Gen. W. S. Rosecrans was assigned to it, the actual transfer taking place on the 30th.

On the first of October our army, rested, reclothed and resupplied, moved out to find and fight the enemy now confronting our lines about Louisville. He retired as we advanced, and passing consecutively through Shepardsville, Bardstown and Fredricksburg, we overtook his rear guard near Springfield, on the morning of the 6th, and our regiment being at the head of our column, we had a continual skirmish all day, both armies moving about seventeen miles towards Perryville, where was a small stream known as Chaplin river. The country we had covered during the past week was almost destitute of water and probably its supposed presence in the vicinity had something to do with locating the collision of the armies at that place. On the 7th we halted in the valley of Doctor's creek, a branch of Chaplin river, in sight of and about three miles east of the village. The creek was nearly dry, only small pools here and there to be found in the bed, and guards were placed over them to prevent the watering of horses and mules in any except those reserved for that purpose.

On the 8th we moved, early in the morning, down the valley toward Perryville about a mile, in search of water, and bivouacked as before, having no tents with us. McCook's corps was on the left of our general line; and about noon we heard musketry, and later artillery firing in his front. No order or information came to us, however, and about four o'clock, our scanty supply of water having again given out, a company was detailed from each regiment of our division, and carrying all the canteens of their regiments, they were sent, in command of Lieut. Col. Bishop, to look for a fresh supply further down the valley to the left. As we pursued our quest we approached the firing and finally found a pool and filled our canteens in full sight of the battle field. One of the enemy's batteries was within easy range of us, but was too busy entertaining their opponents to pay any attention to us. We watched the battle a few minutes and hurried back to our division wondering why the whole army, and especially why our division, was not taking any interest or part in it. Soon after our return, and while the canteens were being distributed, our brigade was ordered to McCook's relief, and moving about half a mile to the left we were posted in a strip of woods, on the right of his line, our regiment so far back in the trees that we could see nothing of what was going on in the front but not so far back as to be out of reach of the enemy's artillery, which now and then landed a shell among us. We were, however, in this position for a few minutes in imminent danger from a line of our own men, a new regiment, which just after dark was moved up into position in the woods immediately behind us. They were nervously expecting to find an enemy in that vicinity, and were just ready to open fire at the first indication of his presence. They could not see us in the gloom, nor we them, but a prompt and vigorous introduction of the two regiments to each other by name probably saved us from what would have been a sad misfortune. We had no experience in the whole war more startling than that cocking of muskets behind us, knowing as we did, that they were in the hands of friends who were not informed of our presence in front of them.

The battle ended with the daylight, but we lay on our arms in position all night and most of the next day, going forward again in the afternoon to the creek valley for water, and there spent the night.

Sheridan's and Mitchell's divisions of Gilbert's corps had got into collision with the enemy's left during the evening of the 7th, in getting into position, and again pending McCook's battle; though separated from him by the whole width of the valley, they had quite a fight of their own, without, however, having any orders from competent authority conforming their operations to McCook's. None of Crittenden's corps participated in the engagement in any way.

As to the battle of Perryville, it was at the time understood that Gen. McCook had undertaken to fight it out with his corps unaided, and failed to accomplish what would have been an easy task for our whole army had all been invited to share in it. The spectacle of his single corps engaged for four hours with the opposing army while our division lay idly within sight of the field, and Crittenden's corps within sound of the guns, is, even at this distance, an astonishing one. It appears from the official reports that neither Buell nor Gilbert knew that a battle was going on until it was too late to put in additional troops effectively, and that Gen. Thomas, who commanded on the extreme right, knew nothing of it until it was all over.

He had heard the firing at a distance, and, sending for information about it, was told that "McCook was making a reconnoisance."

The opportunity to crush Bragg's army was thus lost, and he withdrew it next day.

Our division, now commanded by Brig. Gen. A. Schoepf, included three brigades of five regiments each; our (the third) brigade was now commanded by Brig. Gen. J. B. Steedman, and comprised the 87th Indiana (recently joined), and the 18th U. S., 2nd Minnesota, 9th Ohio and 35th Ohio remaining in it from its first organization.

On the 10th we moved eastward about five miles, passing through Perryville, where we found every house filled with the enemy's wounded. On the 12th we passed Danville and Lancaster, and on the 13th camped on Dick's river at Crab Orchard. Here we remained a week, while Crittenden's corps pursued the enemy southward in a fruitless chase.

During our stay here an inspector general from corps headquarters dropped in one day unannounced, with an order from Maj. Gen. C. C. Gilbert, commanding, to inspect the 2nd Minnesota regiment. The regiment was always ready for inspection, and in a few minutes the column was formed, ranks opened and the ceremony begun.

Each company in turn and the band was critically examined, and notations made of all details. As to the condition of men and equipments no fault was found in any particular; the cartridge boxes and haversacks were all filled, and the regiment could have marched on ten minutes' notice for three days detached service; so the inspector truthfully remarked. The captain of the right company (G) was, however, sharply reprimanded because his first lieutenant stood in front of the center of his company and the second lieutenant in front of the left files, the inspector telling him that he ought to know that these officers should stand in front of their places "in order of battle." The captain replied that himself and lieutenants were in the positions prescribed by the army regulations. The inspector then assumed to place him under arrest "by command of Maj. Gen. Gilbert" for insolence to an officer of the staff. This proceeding was overruled by the regimental commander then present, who instructed the inspector that the captain's reply was not an insolent, but a civil and correct one; that had it been so grossly improper as to justify arrest, Gen. Gilbert had not ordered it, and the inspector himself had no authority to make it. The inspector took his leave in hot anger, saying that we should hear directly from Gen. Gilbert himself.

A day or two later a written order came from corps headquarters for the arrest of the captain to await charges and trial as soon as the convenience of the service would permit. This order was ignored, and next day the inspector, who had made it his business to watch the regiment as it passed on the road, informed the regimental commander that it would be his painful duty to report to Gen. Gilbert that the order had not been obeyed. What might have come of all this, had not the corps commander been so soon relieved of his high rank and command, can only be conjectured.

On the 20th we commenced retracing our march, and passing successively through Danville, Perryville, Lebanon, Campbellsville, Green River and Cave City, arrived at Bowling Green on the 2nd of November.

Gen Rosecrans assumed command, vice Buell, on the 30th of October.

We moved again on the 6th of November, and next day encamped at Mitchellville. The railroad tunnel near and south of this place having been obstructed by the retreating enemy, all army supplies were unloaded from the trains here and forwarded by wagons to Gallatin and Nashville. Our brigade performed this work here until the 12th, when we removed to the tunnel, and for a change of employment spent ten days in guarding and clearing it out.

On the 23rd our regiment, with the 35th Ohio and the 18th U. S., marched for Cunningham's ford, on the Cumberland river, southeast of and a few miles from Gallatin, Tenn., where we arrived and encamped on the 25th. We remained here four weeks, guarding the ford and making occasional reconnoisances about the vicinity. We did not, however, come into any serious collision with the enemy. On the 7th of December a Union brigade of new regiments, commanded by Col. A. B. Moore, was attacked and captured by the enemy's forces, under John H. Morgan, at Hartsville, a few miles farther up the river. On the 22nd we were ordered back to Gallatin, and thence about five miles southward toward Nashville. Here we spent Christmas, and were ordered back to Gallatin in great haste on the 26th.

Our brigade spent the next three weeks pleasantly encamped near the village, occupying a good part of our time in battalion drill and making an excursion into the country now and then for forage and provisions. All day on the 31st of December and on the 1st of January, we heard the rumbling of the cannonade at Stone's river, some thirty miles away, and were glad to learn next day of the Union victory there.

On the 13th our brigade, under orders to join the division at Murfreesboro, marched by the pike some thirteen miles and encamped midway between Gallatin and Nashville. Next day our regiment and the 87th Indiana were again ordered back to Gallatin, and returned in a cold winter rain-storm to our camp ground vacated the previous day, and here we remained two weeks more. This second recall to Gallatin was due, as was the first, to the threatened attack on the place by the Confederate Gen. John H. Morgan. Indeed, for more than two months, we had been shuffled from place to place to meet him, but he never granted us an interview.

During our stay at Gallatin the President's proclamation of emancipation was promulgated, to take effect January 1st, 1863, and hastened the complete desertion by the negroes in that vicinity, of their old homes and masters.

One of these late "contrabands," now freedmen, came to our regimental headquarters with information, that at a point on the south side of the Cumberland river, a few miles distant from our camp, a good many thousand hogs had been killed and cured in hams and bacon in the fall of 1861, for account of the Confederate government; that on Buell's approach in the spring of 1862, the meat had been transported to Nashville and thence to the South, but that the lard in barrels had been buried; that he helped to do it and was willing to guide us to the place. Next morning, Lieut. Col. Bishop, with six companies of the 2nd Minnesota and a section of artillery, went after the lard with wagons to bring back the booty if successful. A march of four or five miles brought us to the river, which was too deep to ford, and the swift current had destroyed the landing so that although we found a flat scow, that had been used as a ferry boat, it was impossible to cross the wagons or artillery. Leaving these on the north bank with one company to protect, if need be, our return crossing, five companies went over in the scow, making several trips with about thirty men at each load, and after marching about a mile and a half our guide pointed out a large field, and said "dar it is." A crop of corn had been grown and harvested there in 1862, but on probing the ground near the middle of the field with our ramrods, we soon located the lard mine. We had brought shovels, and the crowd of darkeys who had joined us, some from camp and some from neighboring farms, very willingly helped to resurrect the barrels which were buried side by side about two feet deep in long continuous graves. Squads were sent meantime to all the neighboring farms, who "borrowed" all the wagons, carts, mules, horses and oxen that could be found, and the lard barrels were conveyed to the river bank as expeditiously as possible.

About a hundred barrels were so delivered, when the ground became so soft from the rain which was copiously falling that further transportation out of the corn field was impossible. Returning to the river we recrossed with twenty or thirty barrels, which were boosted up the north bank, loaded into our wagons, taken to the camp and distributed to the troops and hospitals.

Lieut. Waite was left at the river with a small detachment to load the remainder of the barrels into the scow, navigate it down the river to Nashville and deliver the lard to the depot quartermaster there, which he successfully accomplished.

This excursion served to break the monotony of waiting for Morgan, and as we had plenty of flour the old time doughnuts displaced the hard tack for a day or two.

On the 29th we were again ordered to join our division, and, boarding a railroad train at Gallatin, succeeded in getting to Nashville without recall or interruption.

Our wagons, with our baggage, tents, etc., did not reach us until noon on the 30th. On the 31st we encamped eleven miles south of Nashville, on the Nolensville pike, and under the orders of Brig. Gen. James B. Steedman, now commanding the division, were ready for a new and we hoped more active campaign.

CHAPTER VII.

TRIUNE AND TULLAHOMA.

On the 1st of February our brigade marched in hot haste ten or twelve miles, over the rough, narrow, dirt roads towards Franklin, to encounter Wheeler's brigade of Confederate cavalry, which was reported to be in the vicinity, but we failed to find any enemy, and after a day of hard marching we spent a cold night without tents or shelter. Next day we retraced our path to the Nolensville pike and encamped on the farm of Col. Battle of the 20th Confederate Tennessee regiment, near Concord church, and about twelve miles from Nashville.

This 20th Tennessee was the regiment opposed to ours in the fight across the fence at Mill Springs, and we occupied their camp and tents at Beech Grove the two days succeeding that battle. Col. Battle was now with his regiment in Bragg's army. His wife and daughters and the widow of his son (who was killed, a Lieutenant in his father's regiment, at Shiloh) were at home. We encamped our regiment in the ample lawn, which, shaded with fine large trees and sloping from the house towards the south, was as pleasant a site as could be desired.

Our headquarter tents were set quite near the house and we soon became acquainted with the ladies. They urgently objected to our encamping on the ground we had selected, they deeming any of the flat wet fields farther away quite good enough for us, but being informed of our interview with Col.

Battle and of his kind hospitality towards us a year before, and being reminded that if we did not occupy that lovely lawn some other, and no doubt worse regiment would, they did not further oppose us, though they graciously expressed the hope that our stay would be short. We remained here a month, however, employing our time in various reconnoitering and foraging expeditions towards the front, which always developed an active enemy within a few miles.

Two or three days after our arrival here, Capt. Curtis, of Gen. Rosecrans' staff, made a thorough and critical inspection of the regiment, and soon afterwards a complimentary letter was received from Department Headquarters which referred to the inspection and greatly pleased the men, who well deserved it. (See *appendix No. 13*.)

Col. George, who had been for several weeks physically unfit for active duty and exposure to the severe winter weather, was obliged to leave us here on the 2nd of February, going to Minnesota for rest and treatment, on sixty days "sick leave."

On the 15th a foraging party of two corporals and twelve men, under First Sergt. L. N. Holmes, all of Company "H," went out to the front three or four miles for corn. They were loading their wagons from a large and well filled crib when they were suddenly surrounded by two companies of Confederate cavalry, numbering about 125 men. The cavalry charged down upon them firing their carbines and yelling "surrender you d——d yanks." Our boys in the crib did not think it necessary to surrender, but commenced firing in return, with deliberate aim, emptying a saddle with almost every shot, and the astonished cavalry soon quit yelling and withdrew out of range for consultation; then decided that they had had enough of the "d——d yanks" and disappeared altogether. Our boys filled their wagons, picked up three of the wounded rebels and seven riderless horses which the enemy had left in the field, and returned safely to camp. Two of the wounded died next day. Several others, slightly wounded, got away by the help of their companions.

Col. Van Derveer, commanding the brigade, was much elated by the brave conduct of the 2nd Minnesota boys, and issued a special order complimenting them by name. (See *appendix No. 14.*)

General Steedman, commanding the division, thought the affair sufficiently creditable to "my command" to justify a special report by telegraph to department headquarters, describing the fight; refraining, however, from any mention of the names or regiment of the men engaged. (See *appendix No. 15.*)

Another of these details from our regiment brought in one day eight army wagon loads of fine potatoes, which were a very welcome addition to our somewhat too regular bill of fare.

On the 2nd of March we said "good-by" to our friends, the ladies of the Battle family, expressing our willingness to take any message they might wish to send to the Colonel, and to deliver it, if he would wait somewhere long enough to get it, "as he probably wouldn't," and in return we were invited to stop and see them as we returned northward, if we had time, "as we probably wouldn't."

We marched southward about 15 miles to Triune, where the brigade bivouacked for the night and remained most of the next day.

At 4 P. M., on the 3rd, Lieut. Col. Bishop was ordered with the 2nd Minnesota regiment, a section of artillery and two battalions of the 1st East Tennessee cavalry to move southward to the Harpeth river and take and hold the ford where the Nolensville-Eagleville pike crossed it, and to there await the coming of the brigade, which would follow next morning. The place was reached about sunset; the rebel pickets were driven away, the infantry and artillery were posted to command the ford, and one battalion of the cavalry was sent across the river to reconnoiter the neighboring territory. They soon found some rebel cavalry in small parties, and after a running fight returned towards morning with some prisoners. General Steedman came up in the morning with the other regiments of the brigade, and, crossing the river, we found and attacked a party of the enemy, capturing 60 prisoners and 300 horses and mules. Next day we made a quick march of eighteen miles to Chapel Hill, where we had another brush with the enemy, routing him at the first attack, then returned by another road six or seven miles and bivouacked, marching next day back to Triune, with our booty and prisoners.

On the 7th we made a permanent camp about two miles north of Triune, in a good defensible position with plenty of wood and water.

Triune was a small hamlet about midway between Murfreesboro and Franklin. Here our division was assembled and the first regiment of East Tennessee cavalry was attached to it, and here we remained more than three months. Considerable work was done in fortifying the position, large details being made from the regiments in turn for the purpose. The detail of a hundred men from our regiment quite astonished the Captain of Engineers who had charge of the work, by doing about twice as much as had been done by any previous one. He profusely complimented the officers and men for their efficiency, and to further show his appreciation of their work, he invited the entire detail to division headquarters to receive a ration of whiskey. Arriving there he was embarrassed to find that the commissary had none to issue, and he was trying to frame a suitable expression of his regret, when it occurred to him that Gen. Steedman, who was absent at the time, had a keg of the juice in his tent. Relieved by the happy thought, he got out the keg and a little tin cup, and the boys formed in single file around the headquarters tents; as they passed the keg each one received his ration, and passing around the tents took his place again at the foot of the line. When the keg was emptied some fifteen or twenty of the boys were still in line ready for their third ration; most of them, however, had been satisfied with the second. The Captain, who had taken a ration or two himself, was very sorry there was not enough to go around, but had done the best he could to give each one a drink, and could do no more. The detachment made a somewhat boisterous and disorderly march back to our camp, and their unusual hilarity had to be explained by the officer in charge. It was said that the Engineer Officer was prudently absent himself when Gen. Steedman returned to find the keg empty.

On the 25th and 26th of March our brigade made another excursion into the enemy's territory south of Harpeth river, and after a successful skirmish loaded our train with forage and returned to camp. On the 29th of March we received Enfield rifles to replace the guns of various kinds and calibers which we had thus far used. The Enfields were not satisfactory, but the change was some improvement.

Gen. J. M. Scofield here superseded Steedman, as division commander, and gave us several weeks of pretty active exercise in brigade maneuvers and drill, the first we had ever had.

Gen. J. M. Brannan relieved Scofield May 10th, and continued as our division commander until the reorganization of the army after Chicamauga.

Our bugle band had, as opportunity was afforded for practice, so improved their time that we had become quite proud of them, and having some money in the regimental fund, a complete set of brass instruments was ordered from Cincinnati and arrived on the 8th of April. Principal musician R. G. Rhodes was announced as band master, and for the next few weeks the woods about the camp were full of practicing musicians. They made rapid progress, and before we left Triune, June 23rd, our band compared well with any in the division.

Col. George returned on the 31st of March, not physically in good condition, but able to do duty not requiring active exercise.

Brigade exercises were continued under Gen. Brannan, and a grand review of the troops was held on the 5th of April.

On the 1st of May we were supplied with the new "shelter tents" or "pup tents," as they were called by the men, and all the wall and bell tents were sent back to Nashville, except those required by the brigade and regimental headquarters and for the field hospitals. These pup tents were simple pieces of light canvass, each about the size of an army blanket, and so fitted that two comrades by buttoning their two pieces together and improvising some simple support, could have a comfortable shelter from rain or sun. These tents were to be carried by the men, and so the wagon trains were reduced from thirteen wagons to three for each regiment; the officers of each company being allowed one pack mule to carry their baggage.

On the 4th of June Gen. Gordon Granger came to Triune to inspect the position and the troops which had come under his command as part of the "right wing." The day was spent in brigade and division maneuvers in the hot sun, with little rest and no food or water. It closed with a grand review, after which the troops were marched back to their camps.

Artillery firing had been heard during the afternoon in the direction of Franklin, and when our brigade was dismissed from the review, at 5 o'clock, it was ordered to march immediately to Franklin. Col. Van Derveer, commanding it, gave us thirty minutes in camp after arriving there for supper. During this interval the officers of the 2nd Minnesota called in a body at headquarters and presented a spirited and beautiful bay mare to Lieut. Col. Bishop, who had recently lost his horse by overheating in the field exercises. This presentation was a grateful surprise to him at the time, and and will be gratefully remembered as long as he lives. She proved to be a most valuable and intelligent animal and became a great pet in the regiment. She was twice shot under her rider, but served until the final muster out of the regiment and died in the Colonel's care some fifteen years thereafter.

We marched at 6 o'clock for Franklin, fifteen miles distant. The day had been excessively hot and sultry, but now the sky grew black, and, after a severe thunder storm, it settled down for a steady, heavy, all-night rain. That night's march will never be forgotten by the men of Van Derveer's brigade. The darkness was intense, the road soft, slippery and so uneven that some of the men were down or falling all the time. We were ten hours in making the march, arriving before daybreak utterly exhausted, and physically and mentally exasperated. The garrison seemed to be all asleep. No enemy was in the neighborhood, and we lay down in a lawn in the village to wait for dawn. Our field officers stretched themselves on the floor of the front porch of the spacious mansion.

A little before sunrise the front door opened and a staff officer came out, and waking Col. George with his foot, told him that the presence of the regiment on the premises was not agreeable to the lady owner, and requested him to move on and out. The Colonel had a talent for vigorous and emphatic profanity upon occasion, and he did his best here; but, as he afterwards acknowledged, no man could do justice to such hospitality as that. The officer who had aroused him slunk back into the house, withered and abashed, and did not appear again during the forenoon. In the afternoon we made a reconnoisance in search of the enemy, but found none. On the 6th we returned to our camp at Triune.

The usual round of guard and picket duty, battalion and brigade exercises, was resumed, varied by an occasional march to Nashville or to the front for supplies.

On the 23rd we broke camp on an hour's notice, and commenced the "Tullahoma Campaign"; marching southward and then eastward, in all about fifteen miles, over a rough and rocky road, to a camp near Salem. Here it commenced raining, and of the next seventeen days, fourteen were rainy. Of course the roads and country soon became almost impassable, and the soldiers seldom had dry clothes or rations.

On the 24th our trains moving eastward were threatened from the south by the enemy's cavalry, and Lieut. Col. Bishop, with four companies of the regiment, was detailed to keep them back. We had a skirmish fight in the rain, lasting nearly all day, bivouacked on the disputed field at night, and rejoined the regiment next day. Lieut. Col. Bishop and several of his men got bullet holes in their clothing, but no more serious casualties; the enemy, firing mostly from horseback, did not aim with much precision. On the 29th our regiment had another all day skirmish fight, killing several and wounding others of the enemy. Among the killed was Col. Starnes, and an aid to Gen. Wheeler, who was shot while carrying a dispatch from his chief. After he fell from his horse he was seen to tear in pieces the message, but it was recovered, put together and read. Only one man of our regiment was wounded.

At times, when we had forced back the enemy's line more rapidly than they approved, they opened on us with artillery to check our advance. The surgeon of the regiment on our right, who was riding behind the advancing line, was very suddenly let down by a shell from the enemy's battery, which entered the breast and exploded in the body of the horse without hurting the doctor. The boys unmercifully guyed him as he gathered up his saddle and went to the rear.

On the 26th we had a rattling skirmish for the possession of Hoover's Gap. The enemy gave way for us as we advanced rapidly through the gap, and although they did a good deal of wild firing, no men were hurt in our regiment.

On the 1st of July we drove the enemy's picket line into and through Tullahoma, to find that his army had evacuated the place during the previous night, leaving a good many of their tents standing, several big guns, and a considerable quantity of stores. On the 2nd we reached Elk river, finding it at flood height and the bridge gone. Our regiment captured one party of eleven prisoners, and another of four.

On the 3rd of July the flood had subsided a little and it was found practicable to ford the stream by the aid of a rope stretched across to keep the men from being carried down by the current. Our brigade stripped to the skin; the knapsacks, clothes, rations, cartridge boxes, etc., making a bundle of twenty-five or thirty pounds, were carried on the bayonet, the gun supported by one hand while the other kept a grasp on the rope, as the men in single file waded the stream in the rushing waters up to their necks. None of the men in our brigade were drowned, but some of them lost their bundles in the passage and landed destitute and naked. As the flood subsided the artillery and trains began to cross and a bridge was improvised. On the 4th we heard of the battle of Gettysburg and next day of the surrender of Vicksburg, both events being announced in general orders, and honored by national salutes by the artillery.

The enemy had now disappeared from our vicinity, and as it was nearly impossible to move artillery or trains we rested here nine days, and on the 18th moved to Winchester, where we remained four weeks, the time being occupied in rebuilding the railroads behind us and refitting and equipping for the next advance. Just a year ago we were encamped here for several days, and we now felt quite at home and acquainted.

JAMES GEORGE, COLONEL.
March 21, 1862 to June 29, 1864.

CHAPTER VIII.

THE CAMPAIGN AND BATTLE OF CHICAMAUGA.

On the 16th of August our pleasant camp at Winchester was broken up and we marched eastward about a mile, under a blazing sun, and two miles farther in a terrific thunderstorm; then finding the road full of troops and trains entitled to precedence we encamped. Next day we marched three miles farther, reaching the foot of the Cumberland mountain range, over which our route lay to reach the Tennessee river.

Here we found the heavy wagon trains toiling up the steep, narrow, tortuous road, ascending the western slope of the mountain, and the slow progress of the last two days was explained.

On the 18th we found the road clear, and marched up the mountain side to University Place, on the summit, where we spent the night. Here the corner-stone of a magnificent "to be" university had been laid by Rt. Rev. Bishop Polk, now a general in the Confederate army. An endowment of three million dollars had been pledged, and the foundations of the several buildings had been constructed, when the war interrupted the enterprise with an adjournment "*sine die.*"

On the 19th we marched down the eastern slope of the mountain range, and encamped at the foot in Sweden's Cove, remaining there the 20th.

Since leaving our Winchester camp we had found plenty of green corn, and the "roasting ears" had made a considerable item in our subsistence.

On the 21st we moved to the north bank of the Tennessee river, at the mouth of Battle Creek, about six miles above Bridgeport, where the railroad bridge had been destroyed, and was being rebuilt by our engineer forces.

The river here was broad and deep, and the enemy's pickets lined the south bank. They, for the first few days, kept popping their guns at our men whenever they approached the river, and occasionally the bullets would reach our camps, but we picketed the north bank with better rifles, and after a competitive trial of marksmanship, the men on duty came to an agreement to save their ammunition, and thereafter amused themselves in guying each other "*viva voce.*" The men of both armies, not on duty, came down freely to bathe on their respective sides of the river, and soon it got to be a common practice for a good swimmer or two from each side to meet in mid river and swap lies, newspapers, etc., while the pickets kept watch to see there should be no foul play or breach of confidence.

Col. George rejoined us here on the 24th, from a long absence on sick leave, and left us again on the 27th, promising to be back, if alive, in time for the expected battle. He kept his promise, returning to the regiment on the 18th of September, the day before the battle of Chicamauga. Meanwhile Company "F" of our regiment, composed mostly of river men and raftsmen from the Lake St. Croix lumber regions, had been quietly at work in Battle Creek, out of the enemy's sight, constructing rafts and rude scows, on which four of our companies effected a crossing in the evening of the 29th, and got possession of the south shore. The enemy, not expecting an effort to cross here, had left only a few men to watch the river, not enough to make any serious opposition. By noon next day our entire brigade was over, and the two other brigades of our division (Brannan's) completed the crossing on the 31st.

Meantime the other divisions of the army were crossing simultaneously at several points above and below us, and our trains and artillery were sent down to Bridgeport, to cross on the new bridge when it should be ready.

On the first day of September we moved out about three miles to Graham's Spring, near the foot of Raccoon mountain, and near the monument marking the corner of the three states, Alabama, Georgia and Tennessee.

Near this camp was the celebrated "Nick a Jack" or Salt-petre cave, which was visited and explored by hundreds of our men during our four days' encampment here. A large stream of pure water issued from the mouth of the cave, which was about twenty feet high and seventy feet wide. The cave had been explored, it was said, for a distance of several miles; some of our men, in trying to verify this, got lost, and with considerable difficulty were found and rescued, after spending a very long night, as they said, "in the bowels of the Confederacy."

Here the Confederate government had made an attempt, with some success, to obtain salt-petre for the manufacture of gunpowder. On the 5th, our train and artillery having arrived, we marched up the "Nick a Jack trace," as the ravine is called by which the road ascends the western slope of Raccoon mountain. After making four or five miles it was found that the road needed so much repair and the wagons so much help that it would be impossible to get the trains to the summit that night, and we were obliged to go back two miles to find water for a camp. On the 6th we completed the ascent and encamped on the summit, and on the 7th descended the eastern slope into Lookout, or Will's valley, and encamped at Boiling Springs, about five miles below Trenton.

Here we remained two days, learning on the 9th that Bragg had evacuated Chattanooga on the 8th and was retiring southward.

On the 10th we marched through Trenton and up the Lookout valley about thirteen miles. On the 11th we started in the morning, but having the road ahead of us full of artillery and trains toiling up the mountain, we only made three miles and halted at the foot of a long steep grade. Orders reached us at 7 P. M. to start at once and pass the trains, as the enemy had been encountered on the opposite side of the mountain, but these orders were soon countermanded, and we bivouacked again.

Next morning we started at 5 o'clock, crossed the mountain and halted in Chattanooga valley at 10 A. M. At 2 P. M. made a reconnoisance, returning to our position at 7 o'clock. Here we remained the 13th and 14th, while troops and trains were moving around and behind us in a way that then seemed mysterious and without any definite or intelligible purpose. On the 15th our brigade moved to Lee's Mill, on or near the Chicamauga creek, and bivouacked in line of battle in apparent preparation for a fight right there. We remained there the 16th, "standing to arms" at four o'clock on the mornings of the 16th and 17th, in expectation of an early attack.

On the 17th the heavy clouds of dust extending along the eastern slope of the Chicamauga valley showed us the enemy's columns were in motion northward, and about 8 o'clock we "took arms" and commenced our march "by the left flank" abreast of, and less than a mile distant from, the enemy's parallel march by his "right flank."

Our progress was slow, the day hot and the road ankle deep with fine dust, with which the tramping feet filled the air as the column moved along. At ten o'clock we had got about three miles from our starting point, when some scattering musket shots were heard in our rear, and presently an order was received from Col. Van Derveer, commanding our brigade, for the 2nd Minnesota to return as far as Pond Springs, see what was the matter and rejoin the brigade. We unslung and piled our knapsacks, leaving a few men with them, and in less than an hour retraced nearly the whole forenoon's march. As we came in sight of the springs the two leading companies were deployed forward, and men were detailed from each company to take all the canteens and fill them at the springs as promptly as possible upon our arrival there. Approaching the place we found the springs in possession of a detachment of the enemy's cavalry, who were resting in unsuspicious comfort, many of them dismounted. They had been worrying our trains, and being repulsed by the guards, had halted here for reinforcements. They were promptly attacked and routed by our advance skirmishers, and while we halted, maintaining ranks, the canteens were filled and distributed. Then we reversed our march, returning by the left flank to our brigade, which had not moved during our absence, and soon bivouacked for the night.

The light from the enemy's camp fires was visible all night to the eastward, and we slept "on our arms," ready to be attacked if he so pleased.

All day a feverish, mysterious, nervous foreboding had seemed to pervade the camp; every one was conscious of it and apprehensive that everything was not in order as it should be. The confused and halting marches, of which the purpose or destination was not apparent, were not unobserved by the men, and regimental and brigade officers had little, if any, better knowledge of the situation than their men had.

We remained here all day on the 18th, while troops and artillery and trains were moving behind us to the left or northward, and about 5 P. M. we joined in the procession. Old soldiers will remember that a night march of unusual fatigue generally commenced just before supper. On this occasion we moved about a quarter of a mile per hour through the whole night, halting every few rods just long enough to get stiff and cold, but never long enough to build fires and get warm. Many of the men would fall asleep, sinking down in the road and some standing on their feet, but strict orders were given not to leave the column, and to follow closely those leading us. As the day began to dawn we could see the brigades and batteries leaving the road from time to time and moving off in line of battle into the woods to the eastward towards the Chicamauga creek, and we knew that the army was taking position for the great contest so long anticipated. We could now understand how this had been going on during the night, and how slow and difficult had been the construction of the grand line of battle in the darkness, and our tedious and halting progress was so accounted for.

As we began to understand the situation our vague apprehensions gave place to an active and intelligent interest in the preparations being made, and we braced up and awaited our time for assignment to position. We had been all night in moving less than five miles, were now on the Lafayette-Chattanooga road, and had passed in the darkness near Gen. Rosecrans' headquarters at the Widow Glenn's house. At 8 o'clock our brigade halted, filed out of the road near Kelly's house and stacked arms, while the word was passed down the line "twenty minutes for breakfast." In five minutes hundreds of little fires were kindled and hundreds of little coffee cans were filled with water from the canteens and set to boil by one of each pair of chums, while the other sliced and broiled the bacon; in ten minutes the boiling coffee was lifted off, the luscious bacon was nicely browned, and the ever toothsome hardtack had been moistened and toasted, and—here comes an aid at a furious gallop down the dusty road; a brief order delivered by him to Col. Van Derveer, our brigade commander, and each regiment gets orders to "take arms" and march immediately. Of course some urgent and peremptory necessity was supposed, but how *could* we leave that breakfast untasted, even for love of country or of glory. The bugle call to "attention" was drowned in a tempest of curses, but the order was promptly obeyed nevertheless, arms were taken, and we filed out into the road, now clear, and briskly moved off northward in a cloud of choking dust. "Dreadful! dreadful!" exclaimed our venerable chaplain, as the air grew sulphurous with profanity. "But think," said one near him, "how dreadfuller it would be to go into battle and get killed with all those curses in 'em." "Colonel," said one of these men a quarter of a century later, "d'ye moind that breakfast we didn't ate at Chicamauga? Be jabers, oi can taste it yet."

After making about a mile we halted near McDaniel's house, whence a road, or rather a narrow wagon track, leads through the open oak woods eastward to Reed's bridge and ford on the Chicamauga creek.

It may be here explained that the extreme left of our general line of battle rested in the woods, about opposite the midway point between Kelly's and McDaniel's houses, and the position of the line, extending southward and facing eastward, was about midway between and parallel to the road and the creek. So as we faced the eastward and marched in brigade order of battle along the Reed's bridge road, we were detached from and nearly half a mile to the left of the left division (Baird's) of our established line. Our orders were said to have been given on information by Col. McCook, commanding a cavalry brigade on the left, that only one Confederate brigade had crossed to the west side of the Chicamauga, that he (McCook) had destroyed the bridge (Reed's) behind it, and we were to take and hold the ford, preventing further crossing by the enemy, while our first and second brigades were to find, attack and capture the enemy's supposed isolated brigade. This information, if given, proved entirely erroneous, nearly the whole Confederate army being in position between our lines and the creek, and their brigades were not hard to find when we came to look for them.

Our brigade was formed with the 2nd Minnesota on the left and the 35th Ohio on the right of the front line, with Smith's battery in the road between them. The 87th Indiana in a second line, behind the 35th Ohio; the 9th Ohio was detached with the division ammunition train. So we commenced our march, a few skirmishers preceding our front line. After proceeding along the road, which seemed to follow a ridge of small elevation, and while yet to the left and rear of Baird's division, of whose position we had no knowledge, we heard musketry to our right and front. Changing our direction to face it, to the southward, we moved off the ridge and down an easy slope, and soon met the enemy in force, now supposed to be Echol's and Wilson's brigades, and the firing began at once. In a few minutes the enemy retired, then rallied and attacked again, and were again repulsed, this time retiring out of our sight. We gathered up our wounded men and carried them back over the ridge to the northern slope in our rear (the band performing this service), replenished the cartridge boxes and readjusted our line, the 87th Indiana meantime changing places with the 35th Ohio, on our right. In a few minutes the firing again broke out in our front, but while bullets dropped in among us, we were, on account of the trees and under brush, unable to see any men for a time. Then the firing approached and the big guns joined in for a few rounds, then a burst of cheers, "the rebel yell," the artillery ceased and the rattling musketry came nearer and the bullets thicker. Our men were getting nervous and were ordered to lie down and hold their fire until they could see the enemy. Presently, to our astonishment, a straggling line of men in our own uniform appeared, then more of them, running directly toward us, their speed accelerated every moment by the yelling and firing of the exultant enemy behind them. Our men got ready and waited while the stampeded brigade, officers and men, passed over our lines to the rear, and then as the pursuing enemy came in view, gave them a volley that extinguished their yelling and stopped their advance. They rallied, however, and stood for a few minutes receiving and returning our fire, then wavered, broke and ran out of sight. Just now the 9th Ohio arrived, having abandoned the ammunition train when the firing broke out, and followed our trail to the front. The firing had ceased when Col. Kammerling rode up and vociferously demanded "where them Got tam rebels gone;" some one pointed in the direction they were last seen, and away went the 9th Ohio over our front line, disregarding Van Derveer's orders to come back, and we could hear them yell and cheer in both languages long after they disappeared from sight. About a quarter of a mile distant they found and recaptured the battery (Guenther's), which the enemy had taken half an hour before. The enemy's troops about the battery made a fight for it, and Kammerling lost a good many men in getting it, and was even then obliged to leave it, when recalled by a peremptory order to rejoin the brigade, which he did not receive or obey too soon.

During the first fighting our band men, as they had been previously instructed, were busy with the stretchers, picking up the wounded and carrying them back up the slope of the ridge and over to the north side, where our surgeon, Dr. Otis Ayer, had established a temporary hospital, and was giving them such attention as circumstances permitted. It soon happened, however, that some of these men were shot the second time while being carried back, and the carrying was suspended until the firing should cease.

Our skirmishers soon reported the enemy moving around our left flank, and our regiment by facing left and filing left, changed front to face the east. The enemy made an attack upon us in this position, which was repulsed by our regiment alone, and then by the same maneuver we changed front again to face the north, the enemy having passed a large force around our left flank during the last attack, which was probably made to cover their movement.

We were now in the road again, and on the right of our brigade, on a line nearly parallel to our first position, but facing the opposite direction, and the movement had brought our left company next to the battery, which, without changing position much, had exchanged the places of its guns and caissons, and now faced the north; the other regiments of our brigade had formed on the left of the battery, and for a moment of silence we awaited the onset. Here on the ground, now before us, lay our wounded men, who had been carried back from the first line of fight, and were now between the opposing lines. But—here they come—ranks after ranks—emerging from the sheltering trees and underbrush, and approaching us with steady tramp and desperate silence. Our men were cautioned now to shoot to kill, and we opened with file firing that soon broke up the orderly march of the first line, whose men hesitated and commenced firing wildly; their second lines were now promptly moved up, and all together pressed on in the charge. Our big guns were loaded with canister, which opened great gaps in the enemy's columns at every discharge, while the withering fire of our infantry was thinning their ranks at every step of their advance. They greatly outnumbered us, and it seemed a question for a time whether we could so reduce their numbers and their nerve as to prevent an actual collision in which they would have the majority; but they began to waver at sixty yards, and at forty they broke, and then ran, every man for himself, leaving, alas! hundreds of brave fellows prostrate in helpless suffering before us, some of them intermingling with our own wounded men who had been carried there from the first fight of the morning.

We supposed this attacking force to have been the division which had earlier in the day successfully assaulted the brigades of King and Scribner, capturing their two batteries. This assault and repulse ended our part of the battle for the day; we now refilled our cartridge boxes, gathered our wounded men and sent them to the field hospital at Cloud's house, and collected our dead for burial.

Our regiment had commenced the battle with three hundred and eighty-four men and officers, of whom eight had been killed and forty-one wounded; *none missing.*

While waiting orders here we heard from time to time the roar of battle along the line to the southward, but saw nothing more of the enemy in our vicinity.

In the afternoon we were moved southward to a field southwest of Kelly's house, where we bivouacked for the night. We had had no rest and but little food since noon of the 18th. The night was clear and cold, and many of the men in the excitement and changing positions in the battle, had lost their knapsacks and blankets. No fires were permitted until after sunrise next morning, and we passed a cheerless and uncomfortable night. Yet when we remembered the thousands of poor fellows who, maimed and suffering, lay scattered all over the fields and woods, without food, water or care, we forgot our own discomfort in pity for the wounded and dying.

We all knew that the issue had not been decided, and that the battle must be renewed next day, with probably better preparation and more desperate fighting, and no one could predict what would be his own fate when the contest should be over.

Sunday morning, the 20th, the sun rose peacefully over the misty landscape; all was quiet as the grave; the stillness was in fact oppressive for a time. The tired soldiers, stiff with cold, got up from their hard beds on the ground, stamped the kinks out of their legs and answered the roll call, and then, kindling their little fires, cooked their bacon and coffee. Our brigade, not being in line, was then formed as a reserve in an open field near Kelly's house, and west of the Lafayette road, perhaps a quarter of a mile in rear of the line of battle which, located in the woods, was invisible to us.

About nine o'clock a scattering fire of musketry ran along the line in our front, increasing rapidly until within a few minutes the terrific roar of file firing was in full volume, and the enemy's bullets were passing over our line of battle, chipping through the leaves and branches of the trees, and dropping into, among and around us in a very disquieting manner. Directly the artillery opened also, and while the big shells were not so numerous as the little bullets, they commanded more deference and respect individually when they did come. This did not appear to be a nice quiet place for a reserve brigade, but there was none more sheltered in the vicinity, so we had to stay there and take it; the men meanwhile bracing each other up with jokes and facetious comments on everything in sight or that might happen.

Presently the stragglers appeared coming out of the woods and crossing the road and field, passing us to the rear. Some few of them were wounded, but the most of them were cowardly skulkers who had sneaked out of the line of battle, and were getting out of personal danger as fast as they could. Their number increased rapidly, until it seemed to us that our experience of the previous day was about to be repeated. Some efforts were made to stop and reform the demoralized fugitives, but most of them had thrown away their guns and all of them their courage, and in their then condition they were not worth stopping. One party of six emerged from the woods, carrying a blanket in which lay a man with face covered. These men all carried their guns also, and we set them down as a guard detailed to carry back some general officer, desperately wounded no doubt; who could he be? Possibly our own Van Cleve, whose division we knew was somewhere in the front line. Directly a shell came howling through the woods and burst on the ground near them, when they dropped the blanket and their guns and took the double quick to the rear, and the man in the blanket got up and ran after them. Out of this and other incidents we got some diversion, yet the situation was a trying one and we were much relieved when orders came to go to the left of the line to repel a threatened attack there. We moved northward along the west side of and parallel to the Lafayette road some distance, and then changing direction to the right approached the road with our front facing eastward, parallel to it. At this point we passed through a thicket of small pines and other trees, which had obstructed our view to the north and east. Emerging from this we crossed the road in line of battle, to take position on the left of a battery already there. Our brigade was in two lines, the 2nd Minnesota being on the right of the front line, nearest the battery, the 87th Indiana on its left, and the 35th and 9th Ohio in the second line. Before us lay a large open field, bounded on the north by a strip of woods, perhaps twenty rods distant from the left of our brigade. As we halted on the east side of the road and began looking about for the enemy, whose appearance we expected in our front (eastward), the air was suddenly filled with bullets and a line of gray smoke appeared along the edge of the woods on our left and at right angles with our lines. A change of front to the left was instantly ordered, and executed by the left wheel of the brigade. Pending this movement, which was made on the run, we could not return the enemy's fire, and we lost a good many men. The mounted officers seemed to be especially selected, several of

CORRECTION.

The sentence commencing with the fifth line of page 107, should read as follows:

"The wheel completed, our line commenced firing at once, but finding ourselves at disadvantage in the open field we charged up to the edge of the woods, driving the enemy back and then again opened fire on them at short range."

sion. Among these was their brigade commander, Gen. Adams, of Breckinridge's division. It appeared that this division had passed entirely around the left of our line, and was about to attack our left division in the rear, when we arrived and encountered it as above described.

The fighting over for a time, our wounded men were being gathered up and made as comfortable as possible, until they should be removed to the hospital. In the gallop around with the right wing of his regiment in the open field, the horse bearing the writer was shot in the breast, and dropping to her knees dismounted her rider by a flying somersault over her head. She was abandoned there but was found after the fight by one of our wounded men, and they helped each other over the road to Rossville, rejoining the regiment about midnight. After several weeks in hospital both recovered and served to the end of the war.

came howling through the woods and burst on the ground near them, when they dropped the blanket and their guns and took the double quick to the

... we crossed the road in line of battle, to take position on the left of a battery already there. Our brigade was in two lines, the 2nd Minnesota being on the right of the front line, nearest the battery, the 87th Indiana on its left, and the 35th and 9th Ohio in the second line. Before us lay a large open field, bounded on the north by a strip of woods, perhaps twenty rods distant from the left of our brigade. As we halted on the east side of the road and began looking about for the enemy, whose appearance we expected in our front (eastward), the air was suddenly filled with bullets and a line of gray smoke appeared along the edge of the woods on our left and at right angles with our lines. A change of front to the left was instantly ordered, and executed by the left wheel of the brigade. Pending this movement, which was made on the run, we could not return the enemy's fire, and we lost a good many men. The mounted officers seemed to be especially selected, several of them and all of the horses in the brigade but two, were shot before the affair was over.

The wheel completed, our first line charged at once up to the edge of the woods, driving the enemy back, and then opened fire on them at short range. They were stubborn and slow to give way, and after a few minutes firing by our front line, Col. Van Derveer ordered the second line to pass the first and charge them again. This was done, the first line joining in the charge, and the enemy's front was thus broken up and soon they retired, leaving the field and their wounded in our possession. Among these was their brigade commander, Gen. Adams, of Breckinridge's division. It appeared that this division had passed entirely around the left of our line, and was about to attack our left division in the rear, when we arrived and encountered it as above described.

The fighting over for a time, our wounded men were being gathered up and made as comfortable as possible, until they should be removed to the hospital. In the gallop around with the right wing of his regiment in the open field, the horse bearing the writer was shot in the breast, and dropping to her knees dismounted her rider by a flying somersault over her head. She was abandoned there but was found after the fight by one of our wounded men, and they helped each other over the road to Rossville, rejoining the regiment about midnight. After several weeks in hospital both recovered and served to the end of the war.

Presently the crash of musketry was heard again to our right, and as we listened it seemed to be veering around to our rear. As the enemy then had disappeared from our own front, a few men were detailed to care for the wounded until the ambulances should arrive, and we marched away towards the sound of the guns. The enemy soon reoccupied the field we had won and left, and the twelve detailed men with our assistant surgeon, Dr. Otis Ayer, and many of our wounded were made prisoners. As we got into the open field, where we had been "in reserve" in the morning, we were met by an aid from Gen. Thomas, who conducted us to Horseshoe Ridge, so called, near the Snodgrass house. The battle seemed to be trending to that position from all directions and we could see that we were needed there. Gen. Thomas rode down to meet us, and after giving some directions to Col. Van Derveer, sat upon his horse and looked the men over as we marched past him and up the slope of the ridge. Undoubtedly he was glad to see, in this emergency, the regiments, that under his eye, had fought and won "Mill Springs," and he said to the writer that he "was glad to see us in such good order." We did not then know how many troops he had seen in disorder during the day, nor did he know that within an hour's fighting we had just lost more than one-third of our regiment in killed and wounded, yet we greatly appreciated the compliment at the time.

Arriving on the ridge, our regiment took the place of one already there (the 21st Ohio), which had exhausted its cartridge boxes, and immediately had a view of the assaulting columns of the enemy, just commencing the ascent of the southern slope in our front. Ranks followed ranks in close order, moving briskly and bravely towards us. It was theirs to advance, ours, now, to stand and repel. Again the order was passed to aim carefully and make every shot count, and the deadly work began. The front ranks melted away under the rapid fire of our men, but those following bowed their heads to the storm of bullets and pressed on, some of them falling at every step, until, the supporting touch of elbows being lost, the survivors hesitate, halt, then turning, start back with a rush that carries everything with them to the rear—all who escape the bullets, as deadly in the wild retreat as in the desperate and orderly advance. This was all repeated again and again, until the slope was so covered with dead and wounded men that looking from our position we could hardly see the ground. Never was any position more gallantly assaulted or more desperately defended. Meanwhile General Steedman had arrived with two brigades of fresh troops, who came up on our right with enthusiastic cheers and "forty rounds" in their boxes, just in time to meet the enemy's advance on the crest. Our brigade had so far been the right of our line at this place (except three detached regiments), and being furiously assaulted in front, could not have prevented the enemy from enveloping our right flank, as they seemed to have plenty of troops and had discovered that the ridge to our right was vacant. Steedman's arrival and prompt attack regained and secured that ground, and he brought a spare wagon load of cartridges—more precious than diamonds—as many of our men had placed the last one in the gun. The cartridges were quickly brought to the line and distributed, just in time to meet the next attack. This was made by fresh troops, and their advance was only broken up when their foremost men were within ten paces of our line. Some of them came on and surrendered; most of them who ran back were killed or wounded before they got out of range. From five to six o'clock an ominous quietude prevailed. Our cartridges were again exhausted, and the boxes of our own and the enemy's dead and wounded were searched and emptied, and bayonets were fixed when it was found that we had less than two rounds to the man. Another attack was made just before dark, and was repulsed in our front as the others had been, but there seemed to be no contest on the right, where Steedman's line had been, and presently we found that his troops had been withdrawn and that the enemy were groping their way around to our right and rear, and had already captured the detached regiments which had been between us and Steedman. The 35th Ohio was promptly placed to protect that flank, and after receiving a few shots the enemy retired, no doubt in the darkening woods uncertain of the situation, and disconcerted by the loss of their commanding officer, who fell there.

After another hour of waiting we were ordered to move to Rossville by the Dry Valley road, which we did, with empty guns, but without opposition or adventure, our brigade being, as we supposed, the last Union troops to leave the bloody field. Our division commander, however, says as to this in his official reports (just published) that the 68th and 101st Indiana covered the retirement of our brigade, they "being the only troops that had any ammunition whatever." About midnight we arrived at Rossville gap, and forming line, stacked arms and laid down to rest. Next morning at Rossville, a muster and roll call was had, and every man of the 2nd Minnesota regiment of the 384, who commenced the battle of the 19th, was accounted for; 35 had been killed, 113 wounded, 14 captured and 222 were present for duty unhurt. This report attracted the attention of the brigade commander, who, after verifying its correctness, said in his official report of the battle, "It is a notable fact that the 2nd Minnesota regiment had not a single man among the missing, or a straggler during the two days engagement."

It appears from the "official records" just published by the War Department that our (Van Derveer's) brigade was the last organized brigade to leave the field, being followed only by the two detached regiments as mentioned above. Also, that but one (Whitaker's) of the thirty-six brigades of the Army of the Cumberland engaged in these battles, lost so many men in proportion to the men engaged as did ours. This, considered with the fact that at no time during either day did we vacate any position in presence of the enemy, shows that the quality and discipline of the regiments were to be relied on in any emergency.

The bravery and persistence with which the enemy assaulted our line on the Horseshoe Ridge may be estimated when we know that his two divisions (Hindman's and Preston's) lost more than three thousand killed and wounded in their vain efforts to capture it.

No serious demonstration was made by the enemy on the 21st, though our division remained in position at Rossville gap. That day was occupied by Gen. Rosecrans in placing the troops about Chattanooga as they were collected, and in restoring order and supplying ammunition, and otherwise preparing for defence.

Our brigade was ordered in about midnight, and at daybreak on the 22nd was in line at and in front of Chattanooga. (*See official reports, appendix Nos. 16, 17, 18, 19 and 20.*)

CHAPTER IX.

CHATTANOOGA AND MISSION RIDGE.

As the troops arrived at Chattanooga from the Chicamauga battle field, they were formed in a defensive line extending from the Tennessee river above (north of) the town, around by the east in a grand semi-circle, enclosing it, to the river bank below (south of) it, the line being about two miles long. The river sweeping around the town by the west, in a corresponding curve enclosed it on that side.

Our division, being the last to arrive, at day-break of the 22nd, was placed in position near the center of the line and on and across the Rossville road, by which we had come.

A chain of pickets being established about half a mile in front of the general line, the troops began at once to protect themselves in position, by excavating a simple ditch, throwing the earth in a ridge on the outer side of it, and by the middle of the forenoon a continuous intrenched line had been completed. This was from day to day improved and strengthened, and at intervals quite pretentious works were constructed of earth, and supplied with artillery. The enemy appeared about noon of the 22nd, and as they located our picket line, established theirs conforming to it and from forty to eighty rods distant, and then formed their lines and established their camps nearly parallel and about a mile and a half from ours; occupying also the point of

Lookout mountain and the crest of Mission Ridge, and fortifying them.

Here for two months the two armies faced each other; the enemy having its line of communication by rail from Atlanta open and unobstructed, was well supplied with food, while our army, dependent on a difficult and tortuous route from Bridgeport over the mountains, was for several weeks reduced to half rations of food and forage, while clothing and other supplies could not be got through at all. Most of the men had lost or thrown away, in the two days battle, their tents and blankets, and now these were much needed as the cold weather came on. The exposure to the weather and the poor and scanty food, with the confinement in the line of battle camps, rapidly increased our sick roll and filled the hospitals, while for want of forage the horses and mules generally became unfit for any service and many of them perished.

The operations by which the "river line" was opened and the situation improved cannot be and need not be detailed in this narrative, which does not pretend to be a history of armies or of campaigns. Our men bore the want of proper shelter, clothing and food with brave and uncomplaining patience, and with no thought of giving up the position so dearly won and so important to hold.

Meantime we had some diversions, such as they were. For a while the fences and spare houses supplied us with fuel, but these were soon exhausted and all the shade and fruit trees within the lines were next consumed, the ground being cleared quite out to our picket line of everything that would burn. Then it got to be the habit about once a week to force back the enemy's picket line sixty or eighty rods to take in some more trees. This was usually done at the hour when our pickets were relieved by fresh details, the old and new guards joining in the enterprise. The opposing picket lines got to be on habitually good terms with each other, and although the enemy always resisted vigorously any advance upon them, yet, after the brush was over and the new line established, they seemed to bear no resentment, and would permit our choppers and wagons to work quite up to our line of sentinels and within easy musket range without molestation.

The enemy had planted some heavy guns on the nose of Lookout mountain, and would occasionally admonish us of their presence by heaving a big shell into our camps. One of these shells descended through the roof and two floors of a hospital building filled with sick and wounded men, but without harming any one, as it did not explode. Another one burst over our regiment, mortally wounding Sergt. Caviezel, of Company "F," and injuring several others. Soon, however, our camp sentinels were instructed to watch for the smoke or flash of the gun and give warning, and as the shell in its flight was usually visible against the sky, the men could find shelter if necessary. But, for want of ammunition, probably, the enemy did not thus annoy us very often, and we gradually ceased to expect or watch for the "big kettles," as the boys called them.

Here the army was reorganized, and when this was completed we found that the 101st Indiana, 75th Indiana and the 105th Ohio had been added to the brigade, Col. Van Derveer, of the 35th Ohio, still commanding it. In the seven regiments now composing it, he had in the aggregate less men than in the four with which he commenced the battle of Chicamauga, four weeks ago. We are now known as the 2nd Brigade, 3rd Division, 14th Army Corps, Brig. Gen. A. Baird commanding the division and Maj. Gen. Geo. H. Thomas the corps.

On the 19th of October Gen. Rosecrans vacated and Gen. Thomas assumed command of the Army of the Cumberland, and Gen. John H. Palmer of the 14th Corps. On the 20th our reorganized brigade was assembled and re-encamped in a new position, our regiment occupying what was then known as Hospital Hill, about half a mile in rear of our former position, and a much more desirable location. Here we constructed huts, and with the scanty materials available made them as comfortable as we could.

On the 4th of October Maj. Davis, who had been wounded at Chicamauga, left us on sick leave, and on the 16th of November Col. George also started for Minnesota with a surgeon's certificate of disability and sixty days' leave of absence. About the 1st of November the new line of supplies by the Tennessee river from Bridgeport was secured and opened, and soon afterwards full rations and issues of clothing and camp equipage were realized, to our great comfort and relief.

The topography about Chattanooga is peculiar and picturesque at all times. It was especially interesting when occupied by the opposing armies. In the day time the enemy could look down upon us in and about the city from the surrounding and commanding heights of Mission Ridge, Orchard Knob and Lookout mountain, and doubtless amused themselves in their idle hours in watching our movements and speculating when they should close in upon us and capture us. We in turn could with the naked eye trace their intrenched lines and note the location of their big guns and field batteries, and with field glasses could see their men whenever they appeared in or in front of their lines.

But at night, when the grand semi-circle was lighted up with the enemy's little camp fires, whose light was continually intermitted by the squads of shivering, half clothed rebels standing and moving around them, the spectacle was one we never tired of watching. Nearly every evening the signal torches on Lookout mountain and on Mission Ridge were flashing messages to each other over our heads and across the valley. Our signal officers soon picked up their code, and so Bragg's messages were given to Thomas and Grant as promptly as to Hardee and Breckinridge. Occasionally a big gun on Lookout mountain would open out in a flash like the full moon, and then we suddenly became interested in locating the fall of the shell, though the chances were a million to one that it would not strike anyone's particular position. But as soon as the supply problem was solved the preparations for another battle were energetically pushed, until on the 22nd of November all was ready. On the 23rd the Army of the Cumberland moved out by divisions, in battle array, in the open space between the opposing intrenched lines east of the city, the men carrying three days' rations and one hundred cartridges each.

This movement was in plain sight of the enemy of course, but no special preparations seem to have been made to oppose it. Some of the prisoners said afterwards that they supposed a grand review was to take place and others that the "Yanks" were out of wood again and were going to take in a fresh supply. By a quick rush in the afternoon our lines were advanced, capturing the enemy's intrenched lines on Orchard Knob and along the range of hills connected with it. During the night Sherman's army crossed the river above Chattanooga, and next morning got into position for attacking the north end of Mission Ridge, while Hooker's army got ready for an assault on the north end of Lookout mountain.

Hooker's attack was made on the morning of the 24th, and was so successful that about noon his troops appeared coming around the nose of the mountain into plain view from Chattanooga, driving the enemy before them.

Rain and mist soon hid the contending forces from our sight, but we could distinctly hear the musketry and so trace the advance of our troops as the "battle above the clouds" went on. By night fall the mist had cleared away and the two opposing lines could be located and observed by the flashes of the muskets, which lighted the slopes of the mountain like swarms of fire flies. The contest ended about 9 o'clock P. M., and in the night the enemy abandoned the mountain altogether, crossing the valley and reinforcing their lines on Mission Ridge.

Sherman's attack was made about noon and was obstinately resisted. He did not make much progress though he kept at the enemy all day, compelling him to reinforce that part of his line heavily.

On the 25th Sherman renewed his attack on the enemy's extreme right, at the north end of the ridge, while Hooker descended into the Chattanooga valley and directed his march towards the enemy's left, at the Rossville Gap. The enemy in his hasty retreat had destroyed the bridge over the Chattanooga creek and Hooker had to replace it, which delayed his arrival at Rossville until about 3 o'clock P. M.

Meantime the enemy was marching troops northward along the narrow roadway on the crest of Mission Ridge, to strengthen his right against Sherman, and about noon our division was ordered to our left to report to him. After marching about two miles to reach his position it appeared that he had all the troops that he could use, and we were ordered back to form as the left division of the army of the Cumberland, then in position facing Mission Ridge.

Here our brigade occupied the center of the division, the first (Turchin's) being on our right, and the third (Phelps') on our left. Our own brigade was formed for battle in two lines, of three regiments each, with the 2nd Minnesota regiment about three hundred yards in advance and covering the entire brigade front, with two companies deployed as skirmishers and six companies as reserve (companies "E" and "G" being on detached service).

The official report of the regimental commander, written on the 30th of November, 1863, describes the further movements of the regiment as follows, the entire report being quoted here:

"Headquarters 2nd Regt., Minn. Vols.,
CHATTANOOGA, TENN., Nov. 30th, 1863.

Capt. J. R. BEATTY, A. A. A. G. 2nd Brigade, 3rd Division, 14th A. C.

Captain: In response to circular instructions of this date from brigade headquarters, I have the honor to submit the following report of the part taken by the 2nd Minnesota Infy. Vols. in the operations against the enemy during the week commencing November 23rd, 1863.

On Monday the 23rd inst. at 3 o'clock P. M., the regiment marched from its encampment in Chattanooga with the other regiments comprising the 2nd brigade, with three days rations and one hundred rounds of ammunition per man, and was placed in line of battle about half a mile distant from and in front or south of Fort Negley.

The regiment remained in position here until noon of Wednesday the 25th, when with the brigade it marched to the left, taking a position to the east of, and about a mile distant from Fort Wood, and facing the enemy's positions at the foot of and on the crest of Mission Ridge.

Here the regiment was advanced with two companies deployed, for the purpose of covering the brigade in its formation and movement towards the enemy's works.

The brigade being formed, a general advance was commenced at 3 o'clock P. M. and continued for a distance of about three-fourths of a mile without opposition, when the deployed companies reached the eastern or further edge of a strip of woods and came in full view of the enemy's works; the remaining companies being about 150 yards in rear of the deployed line and the remaining six regiments of the brigade about 300 yards still further back and partially concealed from the enemy's view by the woods in front of them.

Immediately in front of the deployed line lay an open field, the ground descending for a short distance to a small creek, and beyond it rising gradually for a distance of about a quarter of a mile to the crest of a low secondary ridge running parallel to, and about a quarter of a mile distant from the foot of Mission Ridge. Along the crest of this secondary ridge was a breastwork of logs, occupied as the front line of the enemy's defences by two regiments or battalions of infantry. Beyond it the ground descended with an easy slope, for a distance of three or four hundred yards to the foot of the main or Mission Ridge, which rises thence with a slope, gradual at first, but increasing in abruptness towards the top, to a height of five or six hundred feet. Along the crest of Mission Ridge were the main defences of the enemy, consisting of a breastwork of logs, fully manned with infantry, and with artillery posted on the more commanding points in sections of two guns each at intervals of from one to two hundred yards.

The artillery thus placed swept with direct and crossfire the whole space between the ridges mentioned, and also the open field across which we had to advance upon the first breastwork.

In the valley between the main and secondary ridges were the enemy's encampments, the huts mostly hidden from our view by the smaller ridge and the breastworks in front of them.

The space between the ridges had been covered with woods, but, except the steepest and highest parts of the main ridge, where the smaller trees had been felled and "entangled" as an obstacle, the timber had been recently cut away and used in the construction of huts and breastworks.

After remaining in front of this part of the enemy's line for some twenty minutes, I received an order from Col. Van Derveer commanding the brigade, to deploy my entire command and advance upon the first line of breastworks, to seize and occupy it if possible; if repulsed to fall back on the brigade.

The men were briefly informed of the desperate service required of them, and instructed to withhold their fire, and to move steadily forward until the work was gained, and then defend it to the utmost.

The reserve companies were then deployed and with bayonets fixed the whole line commenced the advance. The enemy opened fire with musketry from the breastworks and artillery from the main ridge as soon as our line emerged from the woods, but in the face of both the men moved silently and steadily forward, across the creek, and up the slope, until within about one hundred paces of the breastwork, when, as the pace was quickened, the enemy broke from behind the work and ran in some confusion down the slope into and beyond their camps, where taking cover behind the stumps and among the huts they opened a brisk fire on us again as soon as we gained and occupied the breastwork.

Our line, now partially sheltered by the work, returned the fire with such effect as soon to drive the enemy out of the valley and up the slope of the main ridge, beyond the range of our rifles.

Our loss in this attack was severe, though probably much less than would have been suffered by troops advancing upon the work in regular order of battle. Fourteen prisoners were taken in this breastwork.

About twenty minutes after the capture of the first work, the brigade advanced from the woods, and on arriving at the work halted for a few minutes, when the order was given for a general assault upon the enemy's defences on Mission Ridge.

My regiment moved forward with the others of the brigade, assembling on the colors as far as it was possible on the way, until in ascending the steepest part of the slope, where every man had to find or clear his own way through the entanglement, in the face of a terrible fire of musketry and artillery, the men of the different regiments of the brigade became generally intermingled, and when the brigade finally crowned the enemy's works at the crest of the ridge, the regimental and even the company organizations had become completely merged in a crowd of gallant and enthusiastic men, who swarmed over the breastworks and charged the defenders with such promptness and vigor that the enemy broke and fled, leaving their artillery "in battery," and barely getting away a portion of the caissons and limbers. Six twelve-pounder Napoleon guns were thus captured by our brigade, two of them by the men of my regiment.

Hardly had a lodgment been gained in the works when the enemy's reserves made a furious counter-attack upon our men, yet in confusion. This attack was promptly met by a charge *en masse* by the crowd, which, after a few minutes of desperate hand-to-hand fighting, cleared the ridge, leaving the place in our undisputed possession, with between two and three hundred prisoners captured in the *melee*.

The captured artillery was turned upon the retreating enemy and manned by volunteers from the different regiments, but darkness soon closed over the field and the firing ceased.

The regiments were assembled, and after collecting and caring for the dead and wounded, we bivouacked for the night.

During the operations here recounted, about 150 men of my regiment, including two entire companies, "F" and "G," were on detached service, leaving but fifteen officers and 170 men, 185 in all, present for duty. Of these, one commissioned officer was killed and three wounded, and four enlisted men were killed, and thirty-one wounded; total of casualties, thirty-nine, or a fraction more than twenty-one per cent of the number engaged. Three of the wounded have since died.

The ammunition expended averaged fifty-two rounds per man. Of seven non-commissioned officers in the color guard, all but one were killed or wounded, the color lance was cut off by a fragment of shell, and the field torn out of the colors by another.

On the morning of the 26th we drew rations for four days, and at noon marched in pursuit of the retiring enemy, a distance of about eight miles, to the crossing of Chicamauga creek by the Rossville and Graysville road, where we bivouacked for the night.

On the 27th, at 4 o'clock A. M., we marched again, passing through Graysville and arriving at Ringgold, Ga., about 10 o'clock A. M., a distance of about eleven miles.

Here an engagement with the rear guard of the enemy was in progress, and we were formed in line of battle in readiness to act as occasion might require.

At noon the enemy retired, and at night we bivouacked, remaining in the same position until noon of the 29th, when we marched for Chattanooga, arriving at 6 P. M., a distance of eighteen miles.

Of the conduct of the officers and men of the regiment, under the hardships and privations of the week's campaign in severe and inclement weather, and with insufficient clothing, and scanty rations, and especially of their gallant bearing under fire in the operations of Wednesday, I am incompetent to speak in terms that would do them justice.

The regiment being brought into action, deployed as skirmishers, there was better scope for individual acts of heroism or of cowardice, than would otherwise have been afforded; while I witnessed many of the former, I am proud to say that none of the latter have come to my knowledge.

A list of casualties is herewith transmitted.

I am, Captain, very respectfully,

Your most obedient servant,

J. W. BISHOP,

Leiut. Col., Com'd'g 2nd Minn. Vols."

The brigade commander, Col. Ferdinand Van Derveer, in his official report states his total force engaged at 1,679 officers and men, and his total casualties at 161 killed and wounded.

Separating the 2nd Minnesota force and casualty reports from those of the Brigade, we find that the average loss of the other six regiments was a little more than eight per cent, while that of the 2nd was, as before stated, over twenty-one per cent. This disparity followed naturally from the brigade commander's judicious plan for the attack, which assigned to our regiment the duty of carrying the first line of breast works "if we could" before exposing the other six regiments to the enemy's fire. Doubtless the aggregate loss in the brigade would have been much greater had the attack been made by the whole force, and doubtless, also, the loss in our own regiment would have been greater and our attack would have failed, had not our men kept their nerve and their wind and their cartridges throughout their steady advance across the open field, reserving all for the final rush and contest.

The brigade commander acknowledged the gallant service of the regiment in the following language, which is quoted from his official report: "Especial credit is due Lieut. Col. Bishop for the "management of his regiment when skirmishing in "front of the brigade, and the gallant manner in "which his command carried the rifle pits at the "foot of the ridge."

There has been a great deal of discussion as to who, if any one, ordered the advance from the first line of breast works, up the main ridge. Gen. Grant is said to have ordered the advance *to* the first line. It is further said that he was surprised and angry to see the general line of battle climbing over the first line of breastworks and moving toward and up the slope, and that he sharply notified Gen. Thomas that somebody would be held to account for it; evidently he did not think the assault could possibly succeed.

When we got possession of the first line we found that while to the enemy, standing in a ditch on their side of the work, it was a breast high protection, to us on the other side, it was only knee high and no protection at all against the musketry and canister that rained down upon us from the crest of the ridge. We could not go back and we could not stay there, and without any definite orders our men began to scatter out toward the front, taking such casual shelter as the stumps and old huts afforded, while working up towards the foot of the main ridge.

While this was going on, and when every one could see that we ought to move at least to the actual foot of the slope, where the enemy's artillery could not reach us except by crossfire, Gen. Baird, commanding our division, said: "Let the men go on up the ridge," and they went; the field officers dismounted, as the slope was there impracticable for horses, and presently the whole Army of the Cumberland hung at the foot of that ridge like a blue fringe a mile and a half long. With what expectancy must Grant and Thomas have watched that slow and toilsome, but sure and steady moving up of that line of battle until they could see the colors planted on the log breastworks along the crest, the boys in blue tumbling over it, and the guns turned upon the routed enemy. The enemy appeared to be astonished and disconcerted at our movement up the main ridge, and they fired wildly, both infantry and artillery, so that after we reached the foot of the slope we had but few casualties. If the defenders had done their duty with coolness and courage, every man of us would have been shot on the slope or driven back to the foot of it.

It seldom happens, however, that two lines of battle face each other with equal nerve and determination; when one line insists on staying or advancing, the other gives way. In this case we wanted that ridge and believed that we could and would take it, and did; while the enemy, having just seen us take the first line, and knowing Hooker's troops were approaching on their left and Sherman's on their right, seemed to be convinced that we would take the crest also, and they lost their courage and gave it up without half defending it. (See *Appendix Nos. 21, 22 and 23.*)

CHAPTER X.

"VETERANIZING."

Having returned to our camp on Hospital Hill in Chattanooga on the evening of the 29th of of November, we enjoyed a comfortable night's rest under shelter, after the week of bivouacking, marching and fighting. On the 30th, Companies "F" and "G," having been on detached service cutting timber for and aiding in construction of bridges and pontoons, rejoined the regiment.

The weather was getting cold and wintry, but with fair supplies of clothing, blankets and food, and with comfortable huts and plenty of fuel, the situation was quite tolerable. The enemy, some twenty miles away, seemed quite willing to let and be let alone. About the 10th of December large details were sent out to the field of Chicamauga to gather and bury the dead, who had thus far been neglected. Major Davis returned from sick leave on the 15th, bringing a well filled chest of provisions for the field and staff mess, and various other luxuries and comforts, which were much appreciated. The "F. and S." of the 9th Ohio were invited in, and we made a jolly night of it.

About this date the announcement was received from the war department that regiments having been in service two years or more were invited to re-enlist for three years, and upon so re-enlisting would be sent home on thirty days' furlough. This announcement was eminently wise and timely under the circumstances.

The three years' term of many of the regiments would expire in the summer of 1864, and it had become evident that the war would not be ended within that term. New recruits and new regiments were coming out slowly, and it had moreover come to be understood that a veteran regiment was, in efficiency, much more than equal to a new and inexperienced one. The proposition was read to the regiment at dress parade, and the men were briefly informed by the Lieutenant Colonel commanding that for himself he intended to continue in service to the end of the war, if he should live that long; that the question of re-enlistment was a personal one, that every man should, with due consideration, decide for himself, and that having so decided, his position should be respected whatever his decision might be, and that there should be no distinction or discrimination made or permitted in the regiment between the men who did and those who did not re-enlist, every man being expected to do his own duty faithfully to the end of his engagement.

The question was taken up by the men, and a good deal of earnest discussion was had among them during the next ten days. They were, after two and a half years of service, perfectly familiar with the restraints and hardships and dangers of war, and were not to be enticed into re-enlistment ignorantly. They longed to return to their homes in peace, but they were as loyal and patriotic as when they first responded to the Call to Arms, and they well knew that their services were as much needed and more efficient and valuable than they were in '61.

While the enlisted men were considering the matter, a question arose as to the intention of the War Department with regard to the commissioned officers, they having been mustered anew for three years at each promotion, many of them within a few months. ("Officers in service whose regiments "or companies may re-enlist in accordance with the "provisions of this order before the expiration of "their present term, shall have their commissions "continued, so as to preserve their date of rank as "fixed by their original muster into the United "States Service." Par. ix, A. G. O., Gen. Ord. No. 191—1863.) The proposition of the government (see quotation above) was silent or at least obscure as to this, and on the 19th the regimental commander visited Gen. Thomas' headquarters to get an explanation. After some discussion he was instructed that no re-enlistment was expected of the officers whose companies or regiments might veteranize, each officer having to serve three years from date of his last muster unless sooner discharged, and he was instructed, in case his regiment re-enlisted, to assign such officers as he might select to remain with the non-veterans and to take the others home with the regiment to be furloughed. Later on, it was held that officers must re-enlist for three years like the men, to entitle them to go home with their regiments on "veteran furlough," and those declining the re-enlistment and furlough would be entitled to discharge, as the enlisted men were, at the expiration of three years from their original enlistment. This ruling, however, was not arrived at until after our departure for the North, and was not made known to us until after our return from "veteran furlough." It made trouble for some of our officers, as will appear in the next chapter.

On the 25th of December the regiment was reported at headquarters as re-enlisted; eighty per per cent (about 300 men) having so decided. This was one of the first regiments in the army of the Cumberland to so re-enlist, but several days elapsed before the proper rolls could be obtained and made ready for the muster out and in, which took place on the 29th of December. Meantime, as the writer was informed, two other regiments were got ready and mustered ahead of it.

The payment of the troops and procuring transportation and other preparations for going home consumed several days. The non-veterans, numbering about seventy-five men, were formed into a temporary company, and Capt. John Moulton, of Company "D," Lieut. H. V. Rumohr, of Company "G," and Lieut. M. Thoeny, of Company "C," were detailed to remain with them. This detachment was assigned to duty, during the absence of the regiment, as provost guard at division headquarters.

On the 8th of January, 1864, the regiment embarked at 3 o'clock in the morning, on the small steamers Dunbar and Kingston, and arrived at Bridgeport in the afternoon, distance about forty miles by river. Here six companies were loaded into box cars of a train supposed to be ready to start for Nashville, and the other four companies were assigned to follow on another train with like accommodations. After a leisurely wait, without any apparent reason for it, the first train started at 11 o'clock P. M., and arrived at Nashville at noon next day; while the next train started at 4:30 next morning, and arrived at Nashville in the evening. This trip without exercise or fire or warm food, in the mid-winter, was a pretty severe one, but we were yet in the war country and going home, and there was little grumbling or complaint.

At Nashville we were quartered in a vacant female seminary building, and subjected to another tedious wait of four days for transportation northward. The boys were, however, comfortably housed and fed, and had liberty to go about the city as they pleased within certain hours. At 7 P. M., on the 14th, a train of empty box cars was assigned to us, in which we had another cold and uncomfortable journey of eighteen hours, arriving at Louisville about noon on the 15th, and were assigned quarters in the military barracks. Here was fire and shelter and food, and the boys were just getting to feel warm and happy again when a detachment of the provost guard appeared, with orders to permit none of our men to go out until we were ready to leave the city. These orders, it appeared, were given by the post commander, in the fear, no doubt, that a regiment of veteran soldiers, just arrived from the field of war, would sack the city if not put under restraint. From our point of view, the proceeding was an outrage not to be submitted to for a moment, and a vigorous protest was entered by the regimental commander, who in reporting at post headquarters, announced himself as responsible for the conduct of his men in Louisville as elsewhere, and demanded for them the absolute freedom of the city with all the liberty that any citizen could have; that none of them should be molested or restrained by the provost guard except for crime or disorderly conduct; that the uniform of a veteran soldier should entitle him to the respect and gratitude of all loyal people everywhere and especially of other soldiers, including post commanders and provost guards. These demands were all fully conceded, after a brief argument, and it is now a pleasant reflection that the conduct of the men was such as to fully justify all that was claimed and obtained for them.

Here all needed clothing was supplied for our midwinter trip to Minnesota, and we took advantage of this opportunity to "turn in" our old Enfield muskets, which we had been obliged to carry since our second equipment. Arrangements having been made for this, we had a parade march on the 17th from the barracks to the ordnance building, carrying for the last time the arms and equipments with which we had fought Tullahoma and Chicamauga and Mission Ridge. Many of the men were loth to part with them, but generally the expectation of getting new and better arms on our return, was agreeably entertained. The arms were stacked, the cartridge boxes unslung and hung on the bayonets, and we returned to the barracks "40 rounds" lighter and feeling perhaps more like "furloughed" men than before. Our orders for transportation to Chicago were here obtained over the Louisville, New Albany & Chicago Railroad upon the assurance of the superintendent that we should have comfortable coaches and a quick passage. He at first thought box cars were good enough for soldiers, but we had had enough of that sort when no better could be had, and now insisted upon proper transportation, as it was paid for and we had a right to it. Finally, we were notified that on Monday morning, the 18th of January, our train would be ready and crossed the Ohio river to the New Albany depot to find a train of box and cattle cars, some of them bedded six inches deep with frozen dung, backed down to the platform for our accommodation. The superintendent was conveniently absent, but he was informed by telegraph that the cattle train would not answer our purpose and that we would return to Louisville and ask for transportation by some other line if passenger coaches were not promptly provided as promised.

The weather was intensely cold, with wind and driving snow, and it was a shameful thing to propose to transport human beings in such weather and in such cars as were offered us.

Some hustling was done for an hour or two and then a message came that the cattle cars were all a mistake and that coaches would be ready in the afternoon, and so we waited. About 5 o'clock the train was made ready and we started in warm, comfortable cars for Chicago, expecting to arrive there next morning. Such transportation as that would, however, have been too good for soldiers, and we found ourselves at 7 o'clock next morning within fifty or sixty miles of the Ohio river. The railroad company seemed to have no wood, no water, no competent employees or superintendence, and we spent all that day and all the next night in alternately waiting in the sidings and in rushing over the main line at six or eight miles per hour. On Wednesday morning, thirty-eight hours from New Albany, our weary train arrived at Crawfordsville, Indiana. We had outlived our going home enthusiasm and jollity, and now only hoped that we might reach Chicago perhaps before we should perish of starvation or old age. Expecting here the customary wait of an hour or two at stations we began to climb out of the cars to shake the aches out of our benumbed legs and help wood up the engine as usual. But,—had we broken into heaven, or what? Here were a hundred genial faces glowing with welcome, a hundred voices cheering the veterans, the air filled with hats and fluttering handkerchiefs. The commander was informed that breakfast was ready in the depot; would he please bring in his men. The bugle called "attention," the ranks were quickly formed, and the regiment marched in and down either side of the long tables loaded with "a feast fit for the gods." The ladies filled the cups with hot coffee, with cream, and smiles and pleasant words, while the gentlemen urged us to "eat hearty, boys, you are more than welcome." These generous and hospitable people had, it seemed, spent the small hours of the cold winter morning in preparing this breakfast and in tracing by telegraph our uncertain approach, so as to have it hot and ready on our arrival.

Nothing could have been more opportune or more acceptable, as since the morning of the 18th we had lived on hardtack and raw bacon, with tank water. Breakfast over, our band played some of the popular army music, while the officers and men said all the gracious things they could think of in acknowledgement of the kind and profuse hospitality; then the commander formally tendered the thanks of himself and his regiment, the boys gave three hearty cheers for the ladies of Crawfordsville, and they in turn assembled on the platform and sang "Rally 'round the Flag, Boys," as we resumed our places in the cars. That Crawfordsville breakfast always has been and always will be gratefully remembered by the old boys of the 2nd regiment as long as they shall remember anything. Our progress thence to Chicago was somewhat more speedy, only 24 hours being consumed in the 150 miles, arriving there on the morning of the 21st. After breakfast at the Soldiers' Home, we started again by rail for La Crosse, arriving there at 3 p. m. on the 22nd, where we were again hospitably entertained. Hence forward our transportation was to be in sleighs by the stage company, but only conveyances for half the regiment were ready; Major Davis, with the band and four companies were forwarded the same, evening, and arrived at St. Paul early Sunday morning, the 24th of January, 140 miles in 28 hours, which was considerably better time than we had made on the New Albany Railroad.

The Lieutenant Colonel commanding, with the remaining six companies, left La Crosse twelve hours later and, except three companies, "A," "B" and "C," furloughed at Winona, arrived at St. Paul Sunday evening.

The ladies of Winona gave a hot breakfast to the first detachment and a supper to the second, and the people of all the river towns along the route improved every opportunity to show the boys they were welcome.

On Monday, the 25th, the men dispersed for their homes, each with thirty days' leave of absence, which time they doubtless enjoyed as they deserved to. Most of the companies had formal public receptions by their friends on or soon after arrival home. Among these was, Company "A," originally commanded by the writer, who was a guest at their reception at Chatfield on the 5th of February, 1864. His reply to a formal address of welcome by Hon. R. A. Jones, is here given as then reported by the "Chatfield Democrat" as an expression made at the time of the spirit that had moved the veterans to re-enlistment:

ADDRESS.

Mr. Chairman, Ladies and Gentlemen:

In behalf of the Chatfield Guards, I thank you for the kind words of welcome with which you have greeted us here to-day. We prize them as expressions of your personal good-will as old friends and fellow citizens, and we value them as they indicate your sympathy with our hardships and your approval of our conduct as soldiers, but more than all we cherish and treasure them up as they assure us that you recognize the justice of the cause and the sacredness of the principles in the defense in which we are engaged.

When traitors in arms menaced and at last openly and wantonly assailed the government and the flag, which from childhood we had been taught to respect and revere, and under which we, as a people, had become great and glorious and prosperous and happy beyond all precedent in history, we could have done no less than to pledge, as we did, our best efforts and if need be our lives in their defense.

After some thirty months of service in the field, a few of the one hundred men whom you sent out with your fervent blessing in the summer of 1861 have returned to you on furlough.

Emancipated for a brief season from the stern restraints and discipline of war, they are to-day enjoying for the first time in all those months, the absolute personal freedom of American citizens.

They have exchanged the privations and hardships and dangers of a soldier's life for the plenty and comfort and peace and safety of life at home; they come from a country whose fields are laid waste, and whose society is disorganized and well nigh destroyed by the blighting breath of war, to their own loved homes, where industry finds employment in all the avocations of civilized life, and where all the virtues and graces that make society a blessing to mankind, are in full and healthy play. While you welcome the returned, honor the absent and revere the memory of those who will return no more, may we who enjoy this brief respite from the arduous duties of the field, find ourselves at its close, encouraged in spirit and strengthened in numbers for the work yet unfinished, by our intercourse and association with you here at home.

Having signified our own faith in the righteousness and ultimate and speedy success of our cause by renewing our enlistment in the service, we appeal to you, to every man and woman who has an interest in society or in the perpetuation of the blessings of good government, to aid us in recruiting our ranks from those who have thus far been spared the privations and hardships of the field. You cannot love your homes better, you cannot value the blessings of peace higher than do we, so long exiled from them.

Gladly would we put off the harness of war and return to our homes and to our farms and workshops. Life in the tented field has not, for us, any such attraction as could induce us to accept it of choice. No, far from this. We have re-enlisted not that we love war, or that we are enamored with the roving, adventurous life of a soldier, but rather because we love peace and would aid in its speedy restoration.

We have seen of war all we desire to see, except the end.

Come, join with us then in the final struggle, which shall, with the blessing of God, crush the last semblance of vitality from the already almost prostrate rebellion.

The rebel authorities are making no provision for any campaign beyond the present one. Every able bodied man within their reach is now by the conscript law a soldier. They are marshaling in the field for the last great effort, all their available forces in the full knowledge that to fail now is to fail completely and finally.

Let us meet them with a like appreciation of the occasion, and before another winter shall close upon us, the military power of the rebellion must be destroyed.

This done, it dies, for it has no longer any sympathy or respect in the hearts of the people it has so fearfully cursed.

This done, and the people emancipated from the cruel and odious tyranny which has so long fettered them, will themselves establish the authority of law and order and give the old flag to the breeze in every state from Virginia to Texas.

While we all say "God speed the day," let each of us acquit himself of his own personal duty in the great work of restoration, remembering that through sacrifice and suffering lies the only road to the blessings we so earnestly seek.

The officers, instead of receiving furloughs, had been ordered to recruiting service, and were aided everywhere by the enlisted men, who all felt interested in filling up the regiment, then reduced to less than half the standard strength.

Headquarters were reopened at Fort Snelling on

the 25th of February, and as the men came in rapidly the regiment was mustered for inspection and pay on the 29th, showing besides the 300 veterans about 150 recruits.

In the afternoon of this day, on the invitation of the ladies of St. Anthony, prominent among whom were Mrs. and Miss Van Cleve, the wife and daughter of our first Colonel, the regiment marched from the fort to that place, where a grand supper, reception and ball were given in its honor at the then vacant Winslow Hotel building. The ball lasted all night and ended with a hot breakfast at 7 o'clock next morning, after which the boys marched back to the fort, eight miles, arriving quite rested and refreshed. That St. Anthony entertainment was another event that still warms the hearts of the old boys whenever they meet and talk of old war times.

Two or three days now came of busy preparation for returning to the front. Aided by the active influence of Gov. Stephen Miller, a complete outfit of new Springfield rifles, of uniform pattern and caliber with equipments complete, was obtained, clothing was issued and transportation ordered. On the 3rd of March the first detachment of 150 men was started in coaches for La Crosse, another detachment followed on the 4th, and the remainder, except the band, on the 5th, all with orders to rendezvous at La Crosse.

After a busy day on the 6th, the Lieutenant Colonel, staff and band, left St. Paul on the morning of the 7th, arrived at Winona at noon on the 8th, where the ladies, who had been entertaining all our men as they passed down, had a warm dinner ready for us. They now requested that the band might remain over night and play for them at a concert to be given in aid of their association relief fund. This request, they were told, under the circumstances could not be refused, even if we had to stop the war to grant it, and the field and staff went on, leaving the band to follow next morning. Arriving at La Crosse, the ice was breaking up, and the crossing was a tedious work of considerable danger and difficulty. It was accomplished, however, without accident on the 9th and 10th, and at 3 A. M. on the 11th we started by railroad for Chicago.

Col. George, who had left us at Chattanooga four months ago, rejoined the regiment here and assumed command. After breakfast in the Chicago Soldiers' Home, on the 12th, the regiment was forwarded in detachments to Louisville, the last arriving there early on the 16th, and after a day's delay proceeded to Nashville, arriving Saturday morning, the 19th. The railroads were crowded with returning veteran regiments and supplies for the army at the front, and after waiting three days we got orders to march through to Chattanooga, and moving out of the city four miles, encamped in the afternoon of the 23rd.

The march was uneventful—an easy one for the veterans, but a new and tough experience for the recruits. We arrived at Stevenson on the 5th of April, and climbing on top of a train of loaded box cars, proceeded thence by rail to Chattanooga, where we encamped on the 6th on Chattanooga creek, and reported our arrival to division headquarters, then at Ringgold. On the 9th we resumed our march, and on the 10th rejoined our old brigade and division at Ringgold, Ga. Here we received a most hearty welcome from our non-veterans, who now rejoined us, and from our old comrades of the other regiments. The 9th Ohio, informed of our approach, and knowing that all the unoccupied buildings in the town had already been demolished to build camps for the troops there, kindly went out the day before our arrival and pulled down a country church, that we might have lumber and brick on our camp ground on arrival.

And here ended our veteran furlough.

CHAPTER XI.

THE ATLANTA CAMPAIGN.

At Ringgold we found the army comfortably in camp. Trains were running pretty regularly bringing rations, forage, clothing, camp equipage and ammunition from Louisville and Nashville, but the daily consumption of so large an army was enormous and the supplies accumulated slowly. Nearly every train brought also, on the roofs of the loaded cars, a veteran regiment returning from furlough.

For us the next four weeks were full of business; we had about 450 men present "for duty," one-third of them being new recruits without any real experience as soldiers except that gained in the march through from Nashville, which was of considerable value in putting them on their soldier legs. These men had to be taught to handle their arms and equipments, and instructed in guard and picket duty and in the school of the soldier, the company and the battalion. They were distributed to the several companies and paired off with veterans as much as could be. Daily drill and exercise, forenoon and afternoon, with dress parade at "retreat" was the regular order, varied once a week by a regimental tour of picket duty in front of the enemy.

On the 29th of April our brigade made a reconnoisance to the front, on which we found and developed the enemy's line, returning, however, without casualties, after giving our recruits their first view of the men in grey. This was repeated on the 2nd of May, the brigade going seven miles to Tunnel Hill.

On the 6th of May the regiments got ready for active work by a careful inspection of men and arms and equipage. The sick and lame were sorted out and with all surplus baggage sent back to Chattanooga, the cartridge boxes always filled to "40 rounds," were carefully examined and the havresacks supplied with three days' rations, and the ammunition and supply wagons loaded and packed ready to follow the troops.

On the 7th the Atlanta campaign began—the famous hundred days of maneuvering and fighting, without an hour, by day or night, of absolute quiet, all over the field of operations. We broke camp at 4 o'clock A. M. and the troops were soon in motion, arriving at Tunnel Hill (driving the enemy's skirmishers before us) at noon. Here the enemy was strongly intrenched and some hard fighting was done without dislodging him, our own regiment not being seriously engaged. Next day commenced the movement of McPherson's corps to the right and through Snake Creek gap to the enemy's left and rear, resulting in his evacuation of Dalton on the night of the 12th. Another three days of skirmishing and a flank movement to the right forced the evacuation of Resaca by the enemy on the night of the 15th.

On the 16th we bivouacked at Resaca, on the 17th at Calhoun and on the 18th passed through Adairsville, on the 19th we marched through Kingston and bivouacked beside the railroad near Cassville, where we remained three days. Here, on the 21st, our long-time comrades of the Ninth Ohio were ordered to Cincinnati for muster-out, their three years' term having expired. Our men had spent most of the day in visiting and saying "good by" to them, and when they were ready to leave our regiment was formed to give them a parting "present arms" as they marched past our front, followed by three rousing cheers for the heroes and comrades of Mill Springs, Chicamauga and Mission Ridge.

On the 23rd we marched four miles, forded the Etowa river, and six miles farther on bivouacked at Euharlie creek. For the next eight days we were in charge of trains in the rear of our general line of battle. On the 2nd of June we were ordered to the front, and coming up to the enemy's fortified lines our brigade intrenched a parallel line in his presence and held it until the 5th, when he evacuated his position. It would be tedious to detail here the alternate moves, waits and fights of the next four weeks. Some part of our army was under fire all the time. So continuous was the uproar of musketry and cannon, near or remote, and so accustomed to it did we become, that we came to ignore it altogether unless actually engaged in it. Our men ate, slept, wrote letters, played cards and chuck-a-luck, washed and mended their clothes and polished their rifles in careless indifference until we ourselves were called out to make or repel an attack. If at any hour of the night the din of war would absolutely cease the unwonted silence would awaken the sleeping soldiers to wonder what had happened.

On the 18th of June it was our turn at the front. We moved at 9 A. M., in the rain, and our skirmishers soon came to the crest of a low ridge in full view of the enemy's intrenchment, about 300 or 400 yards away. It was well filled with infantry and artillery, and they were evidently quite ready to receive us, their skirmish line having been withdrawn to their breastworks. Our ridge commanded the enemy's line, and it seemed important to occupy it. Presently, indeed, instructions came from corps headquarters to our division to establish our line of battle on that ridge if possible, and in due time the order came to the 2nd Minnesota to mark and entrench a line there for our brigade front. A skirmish line was detailed, and the men being carefully instructed by the

Lieutenant Colonel, each one carrying a spade besides his gun, knapsack, etc., moved briskly up to and were hastily aligned along the crest. Then each man lying down flat with his gun by his side and his knapsack at his head, commenced excavating a shallow ditch, throwing the earth up in front and working towards his neighbor. After ten or fifteen minutes of lively work a second detail went out, and, taking the spades, continued the work while the first resumed their guns and rested. The enemy kept up a scattering infantry fire on us, but we were making good progress with no casualties, and would soon have had a continuous line intrenched. Suddenly a six-gun battery came rushing up from behind us, and went into action on the ground we had been intrenching, nearly running over some of our men who were working there. It was a showy, but an unfortunate and unnecessary exploit; did no good, and cost some valuable lives. The enemy's artillery immediately opened on it and on us every gun within range, and, they being well protected while this battery stood exposed, it got much the worst of the fight, and soon withdrew, having lost a good many men and horses and being generally knocked to pieces. Meantime Lieut. Jones was killed and eleven others of our regiment were wounded during the few minutes of artillery fighting, and the work of intrenching was necessarily suspended, the line being close under the muzzles of our battery while in action. It was resumed immediately after the battery withdrew, and the line was completed, but as the enemy continued and increased his infantry firing, we were obliged to deploy a line to reply to it, which was done with such effect as to keep the enemy's heads down and prevent good aiming, so we had but few men hurt by their wild firing.

Gen. O. O. Howard, in the "Century" for June, 1887 (page 454), speaks of this affair as follows, being a witness of the concluding part of it: "Here I saw a feat the like of which never else- "where fell under my observation. Baird's division, "in a comparatively open field, put forth a heavy "skirmish line, which continued under a heavy fire "such a rapid fire of rifles as to keep down a "corresponding hostile line behind its well con- "structed trenches, while the picks and shovels "behind the skirmishers fairly flew until a good "set of works was made four hundred yards off "and parallel to the enemy's."

Our line established, we made it so uncomfortable for the enemy that at night they abandoned their position, drawing back to a new fortified line, with Kenesaw mountain as the centre and key point, and extending from it east and southeast, west and southwest, covering Marietta and the railroad from there to Atlanta. Our army was immediately put in motion and closed up again to within easy musket range of the enemy's new position, our division being located in front of the mountain, on which several batteries had been posted. Our line was intrenched, the usual ditch and embankment being supplemented by a breastwork of heavy logs, which, covered and protected by the earth in front, proved a good protection from artillery fire. All the ground in our vicinity was covered by the guns on the mountain, and for a day or two they kept it so warm with shot and shell as to confine us closely to the breastworks; but, when the enemy got tired wasting ammunition and ceased firing, our little tents were set and the space in the rear and near the breastworks was occupied by our men in comparative comfort, a watch being stationed to give warning whenever a puff of smoke appeared on the mountain.

The enemy amused themselves two or three times a day by shelling our camps vigorously for a few minutes to see the "Yanks" run for the breast works. Here the muster out rolls were prepared and orders obtained for the discharge of our non-veterans, whose three years term was nearly expired. Col. George announced his intention to retire also at the end of his term, and received orders on the 22nd to go to Chattanooga on the 23rd with the non-veterans, there to be mustered out. The Colonel's age and physical infirmity disqualified him for a hard campaign like this, but he persisted to the completion of his term and left us at last much to our regret and his own.

About midnight on the 22nd our regiment was ordered to move about half a mile to the right to relieve another regiment there which was ordered elsewhere. It was a bright, still, moonlight night, and the enemy on the mountain was vigilant and in the habit of investigating with his artillery every suspicious movement, so the men were instructed to move quietly, keeping their gun barrels covered, all verbal orders and conversation to be omitted. Our movement was thus safely made, but, on our arrival, the commander of the regiment to be relieved woke up his men at long range by shouting the regulation commands in a voice that could be easily heard by the enemy, who could also see the glimmer of their muskets in the moonlight, and before his men were ready to move a big round flash was seen on the mountain—a few seconds later another, right in our faces, with a deafening explosion, and six men at the head of our regiment lay mangled on the earth. The going regiment took to the woods without any more formal orders, and our men took their places in the breastworks without any further casualties, though a furious cannonade was kept up for half an hour or more. One of the men killed was our Sergt. Maj. P. G. Wheeler, who a few hours later would have gone to the rear to be discharged. It seemed very sad that after three years' faithful service without injury, he should fall in the last hours of his term.

Next morning at daybreak Col. George and the one hundred and three non-veterans present with the regiment got ready to take leave of us, and with hearty good wishes and good-byes we parted with them "for three years or during the war."

On the 27th our division was placed in reserve to Davis' division, which was ordered to assault the enemy's intrenched line. The attack was most gallantly made, but failed, because the line was too strong and too well defended, and could not be carried. The loss in the attacking division was heavy, but in our division, not seriously under fire, there were but few casualties.

On the 2nd of July a detachment of seventy-eight drafted men joined us from Minnesota, and were distributed among the companies.

The enemy evacuated Kenesaw during the night, retiring south of Marietta.

On the 4th our brigade was ordered to garrison duty at Marietta, where we remained eight days. This was now the grand supply depot for the army, and we had not only to protect the place from probable cavalry raids, but unload several trains a day of army supplies and reload them into wagons for the front. Our regiment was encamped on the beautiful lawn of ex-Gov. McDonald's homestead, and with a comfortable camp, sufficient rations, and no marching or fighting to do, we enjoyed the week here notwithstanding the hard work and picket duty. The new men were meantime kept busy learning the duty of soldiers.

On the 13th our brigade marched nine miles to the front, rejoining the division, and next day another detachment of ninety-eight drafted men joined us. Here recommendations for promotions to fill vacant offices in the regiment were made and forwarded to the Governor of Minnesota. (See *appendix No. 24.*) On the 15th our regiment was ordered back to Marietta to relieve the 20th Connecticut regiment as provost and depot guard. We continued on duty here for five weeks, our time busily occupied in guard and picket duty, in handling commissary and quartermasters' stores and in instructing our 176 new men, who, being mingled in squads with the veterans, made rapid progress.

On the 19th of August we marched again to the front and rejoined our brigade before Atlanta on the 20th.

Now we were again in the enemy's immediate presence and our old experience of marching, fighting, intrenching and maneuvering was renewed and kept up until on the 30th, the final movement around the enemy's left flank began, culminating on the 1st of September in the battle of Jonesboro, fought and won by our 14th corps. Our brigade happened to be in the second line during the fighting, and had but three men wounded, none killed. The enemy was badly beaten and broken up in the battle, and about 3 o'clock next morning the Confederate army evacuated Atlanta, setting fire to the storehouses containing their surplus ammunition and stores which, as we had broken the railroad, they could not move. The racket of exploding shells, distinctly heard at our bivouac, reminded us of the evacuation of Corinth, of which we had like audible notice, and we knew that at last Atlanta was ours.

After remaining near Jonesboro two days we leisurely marched back toward Atlanta, and encamped near the city on the 8th of September. We had left Ringgold on the 7th of May with 451 officers and men present. This number had been increased by recruits 176, returned from hospital or detached service, 67, and had been diminished by killed in battle, 4; wounded and sent to the hospital,

16; sick and sent to the hospital, 113; discharged at expiration of service, 103; deserted, 3; transferred, 2; dismissed, 7, leaving present for duty Sept. 7th 446 officers and men. Not all the wounded went to the hospital. (See *list of casualties Appendix No. 25*.)

While the regiment rests comfortably a few days at Atlanta a bit of unpleasant history may be briefly given. Reference was made in the preceding chapter to the absence of any definite understanding at the time the regiment re-enlisted, as to what was to be done with, or by, the commissioned officers of companies or regiments whose enlisted men might "veteranize," and the instructions given to the regimental commander in our case, under which three officers were by him detailed to remain with the non-veterans and the others, except several sick and absent, were taken to Minnesota with the regiment, and some of them placed on recruiting service during the furlough, on the theory that they would not be held to have re-enlisted. After our return to the front we found that a ruling had been made that officers of veteran regiments who accompanied their regiments home on furlough would be held as re-enlisted from the date of the veteranizing, and officers declining the furlough would be entitled to discharge at the end of three years from the time of original entry into service. On the 16th of June Col. James George applied for the discharge of himself and eleven other officers and one hundred and one enlisted men, non-veterans, then with the regiment (or in the division) whose time of service would expire within the next month.

On the 18th one of these officers was killed in battle. On the 22nd of June orders were received for Col. George with the enlisted men, non-veterans, to go to Chatanooga for muster out. On the 29th, no orders as to the other officers who had applied with Col. George for their discharge, having been received, six of them renewed their request for discharge at the expiration of their original terms (June 26th to July 8th), "or as soon thereafter as the exigencies of the service will permit." One of these men was a few days later wounded in action. Their second request was approved as the first had been, by the regimental and brigade commanders, on the ground that these officers accompanied the regiment to Minnesota on veteran furlough in January last before the order requiring officers to re-enlist, or retaining in the field those who declined to re-enlist, had been received, and upon the further ground that the regiment had been so much reduced by the discharge of non-veterans that the officers desiring discharge after having served their three years, could be now spared.

The response was made to this request that the Department Commander had recommended the *dismissal* of these officers. A full explanation and protest was immediately made, and forwarded through intermediate headquarters to the War Department by the regimental commander. The officers continued in the service, doing their duty gallantly and efficiently, until just after the smoke had lifted from the battle field of Jonesboro, an order was received from the War Department dishonorably dismissing the six officers for "having, "whilst their commands were in front of the enemy applied to be mustered out, after having availed themselves of the furlough granted their regiment as veteran volunteers." This order dated back to July 12th, thus covering with disgrace two months of faithful service in the enemy's presence, after their terms had expired. This order had to be, and was revoked afterwards, and the victims of it were honorably discharged as of such later dates as included the whole time actually served; but it was a cruel outrage that it ever should have been issued, even under misapprehension of the facts, for which they were in no wise responsible.

The remainder of the month of October was occupied with the usual routine of camp life and duty, a great deal of attention being given to our recruits, who were rapidly becoming soldiers. Meantime many of the older regiments were, like ours, becoming reduced by the discharge of non-veterans at expiration of their original terms of three years; and while all the loyal states were raising and equipping additional troops to fill the quotas called for by the President, most of the governors were organizing them into new regiments, which were sent to the front, in many cases, under field and company officers of little or no actual military experience. Such regiments were of little use in active service in the enemy's presence, while if the recruits had been distributed to the companies of the veteran regiments the new men would, by association with the veterans and under the instruction and care of veteran officers, have soon become efficient and reliable. Gen. Geo. H.

Thomas, who had known our regiment, having it under his command for three years, especially desired to have it filled up to standard strength, and about the 1st of October the writer, the Lieutenant Colonel, then commanding the regiment, received a special written request from him to the Governor (Stephen Miller) for the assignment of two hundred recruits with an order to present the requisition in person. Leaving the regiment in charge of Maj. C. S. Uline, he started immediately for Minnesota.

Next day commenced the northward movement of Hood's army, and on the 4th the regiment, with its division, began the tiresome tramp over the familiar ground of the last summer's campaign.

The march was uneventful so far as our regiment was concerned; it arrived at Gaylesville on the 21st, and moved thence to Rome on the 30th, and thence to Kingston on the 2nd of November.

On the 4th our band master, R. G. Rhodes, arrived with a complete outfit of silver horns from Cincinnati. He had been sent from Atlanta for them, with our regimental fund, liberally supplemented by private subscriptions by the officers of the regiment. We were all very proud of our band who had by faithful use of their old instruments well earned the better ones.

Meantime the Lieutenant Colonel, after a tedious trip with many breaks and delays, had been to Minnesota, procured the assignment of eighty-eight men, all that there were then at Fort Snelling unassigned, and had got back to Chattanooga with them, just in time to take the last train thence to the front, arriving at Kingston at eleven o'clock in the evening of November 11th. The train was immediately unloaded and returned northward, and at daybreak next morning the railroad and telegraph lines were broken behind us and the troops started for Atlanta.

Our regiment delayed a little to distribute our recruits and provide them with rations and ammunition, but marched at nine o'clock and rejoined our brigade at Altoona in the evening.

CHAPTER XII.

THE MARCH TO THE SEA.

Our communications northward by railroad and by telegraph had been severed behind us, and leaving our old commander, Gen. George H. Thomas, to take care of Tennessee and of Hood's army, we turned our faces southward and retraced the now familiar way to Atlanta.

On the 14th of November we halted an hour or two at Marietta, where we had been on garrison duty five weeks in the preceding summer. The once beautiful village had been sadly devastated by the passing hostile armies, and our old camps in the shaded lawns were hardly to be recognized.

On the 15th we marched into and through Atlanta, encamping about two miles east of the city. Here we filled our cartridge boxes and haversacks, put on new shoes and clothing, loaded our wagon trains with ammunition and rations of coffee, sugar and hard tack, and disencumbered ourselves of all unnecessary baggage and equipage in preparation for the campaign; of which the direction and the duration were not then definitely known even to the commander himself. The great buildings in Atlanta that had been used by the enemy for manufacturing and storing military supplies, had been set on fire and the conflagration had spread over a great part of the town, there being neither men nor means to confine it. All that night. the burning city lit up the sky, and the exploding shells and cartridges kept up a noisy but harmless cannonade.

Next morning, the 16th, the 14th corps, with colors unfolded to the mild autumn breeze, and bands playing the inspiring martial music, filed out into the road and commenced the now historic "March to the Sea." Never marched an army more confident of success or more competent to achieve it. The men were mostly veterans of three years' service, accustomed to everything that happens to men in war, acquainted and satisfied with their commanders, and well supplied with those essentials not to be gathered in the country.

In our own regiment the veterans and the recruits were about equal in number, but they had been so mingled in the companies and squads, and the new men so well instructed by the veterans, that they were quite competent to take care of themselves and do any duty of the soldier.

Our course was eastward, parallel and near to the track of the Georgia railroad; passing through

Decatur and near Stone mountain, we encamped early, after an easy march of 15 miles. In the next day's march we passed through Lithionia and Conyers. We halted at noon for lunch, and then our brigade wrecked two miles of the railroad track before resuming the march.

This railroad unbuilding was thoroughly and rapidly done, about as follows: Our regiment, having stacked arms and unslung knapsacks near the road, is formed in a single rank outside the track, facing inwards. The rail joints at each end of the line being opened, the men all seize the rail with their hands, and at the "Yo heave" command they all lift together, raising the rails and ties gradually up and higher and finally overturning the entire track. The rails are joined only with the old style cast iron chairs, and in falling on its back the track is shaken up and loosened. The ties are now knocked off and piled upon the road-bed, cobhouse-wise, a few dry fence rails mixed in for kindling, the fire is started and the iron rails being laid across the piles are in a short time red hot at the centre. A lever and hook is now put on each end of each rail, and both ends are so turned in opposite directions and brought down to the ground as to give the rail at once a spiral twist and a Grecian bend along its middle third. Sometimes the boys would give them an extra heating and wind them around the trees by the roadside, and at every mile-post the letters "U. S." in sixty-pound rails were set up to encourage the loyalty of those who might see and read. Our cavalry having broken a bridge some miles ahead of us, we found a locomotive and train of cars at Conyers; they were unable to get away before our arrival—or afterwards.

On the 18th we passed through Covington, a pretty village, and crossed Yellow river; halted at noon for lunch and disintegrated our usual two miles of railroad track.

Resuming the march we halted to rest by the roadside about 3 o'clock, near a spring, where several of our brigades had refreshed themselves in advance of us. Close by was a comfortable farm-house with several ladies in the wide veranda who watched the pranks of the soldiers with much apparent interest. Presently one of the men in our leading company noticed that the sods and earth upon which he was lying had apparently been recently disturbed. Drawing his ramrod he probed the soft spot with the air of an expert and called for a spade. A few minutes of lively work disclosed a pine box while his comrades crowded around him speculating as to what valuables it might contain. The ladies, too, seemed to be excited and anxious about it—perhaps their money or their silver spoons were in peril. The box being carefully uncovered the top was pried off and there exposed to view were the remains of a spaniel dog, rebuking his disturbers with an odoriferous protest that reached their consciences by the most direct route. The lid was replaced, the pit refilled and the earth and sods carefully replaced and dressed over ready for the next brigade. Now the lady of the house graciously remarked that poor Fido was not resting in peace very much that day; this was the fourth time he had been resurrected since morning.

On the 19th we turned southward and left the railroad, directing our march towards Milledgeville. The enemy had destroyed the bridge over Little river and we had to lay a pontoon bridge, which delayed our march an hour or two. The day was rainy and the road slippery, and the marching tiresome and uncomfortable. Next day we passed through Shady Dale, and on the 21st the weather was fine and we made good progress; on the 22nd we encamped on a plantation, owned by Howell Cobb, who had been United States Senator and Secretary of the Treasury, and was then a general in the Confederate army. Here we loaded a spare wagon with peanuts, fresh from the ground on which we had camped; on the 24th we entered Milledgeville, the capital of Georgia, and remained there encamped over the next day, which was "Thanksgiving Day," and was duly celebrated as such.

We had been eight days on the road from Atlanta, and thus far had drawn no rations from our wagon trains except coffee. There had been, however, no lack of provisions; it was in that country the season of plenty; there had been cultivated by negro labor a most bountiful crop of corn, sweet potatoes and various vegetables, and on every plantation were fat cattle, pigs and poultry in abundance, while the smokehouses were filled with hams and bacon just cured.

Butter, honey, sorghum, syrup, apples, home made jelly and preserves and pickles had been also provided and stored for us, and it wasn't even necessary to ask for them. Every morning an officer with a sergeant and ten men (one from each company) were sent out to provide a day's subsistence for the regiment. These details were called foragers and later "bummers." They were of course armed and kept together, and were thus enabled to whip or at least "stand off" any party of the enemy's cavalry they might meet. Details from other regiments, which scattered and straggled, lost a good many men by capture, but not a single man of ours was so lost, either from the foragers or the column during the entire march to Savannah.

These foragers would get as far ahead as they could in the first hour or two, then leave the road and visit the plantations, find a wagon or cart or perhaps a carriage and a single, or pair of, mules or horses or oxen or cows to haul it, load it with corn meal, potatoes, ham, poultry and everything else they could find that was edible, and leading a fat steer or two would return to the roadside, and "join in" the column as the regiment came along. The quantity and quality of supplies thus collected by these foragers was more than sufficient, and the grotesque appearance of the bummers as they lined the roadside in the afternoon waiting to join their regiments, was a never failing source of amusement. They usually went out on foot, but returned mounted or in carriages, in all styles, from a creaking, rickety cart with a single mule or steer in rope traces, to a grand coupe with a blooded pair in silver mounted harness. The officer in charge was always instructed to permit no wanton destruction of property, nor firing of buildings, nor abuse of people at their homes, and as far as is known to the writer these instructions were observed by *our* details, but in many cases, no doubt, soldiers who were unrestrained by instructions or discipline were guilty of plundering and cruelty, not to be justified even in war, though such acts could not always be prevented by those in authority.

During this march it was the rule, as it was in all other marches, that every man should keep his place in the column, straggling being in our regiment absolutely forbidden; this for three reasons; first, for his own safety, for the straggler was liable to be captured or killed, as many were, by the enemy's cavalry, which always followed and hung around our rear and flanks; second, for his own good, that he might arrive in camp and get his supper and rest with his comrades, rather than to fall out, get behind and then have to travel alone far into the night, perhaps, to find his regiment; and third and chiefly, for the sake of good order and discipline—that in any emergency, always to be expected and prepared for in war, the regiment should be ready in full strength, every man in his place.

It was a custom of the regimental commander to look personally to the observance of this rule, and in the performance of this duty he noticed one day one of the recruits who, loaded with his gun and forty rounds, his canteen, haversack, blankets and a big knapsack, was bravely tiptoeing along on his sore feet with his company. A word of encouragement to him brought forth the response "the spirit indeed is willing but the flesh is weak," yet he hoped to keep his place, for he well knew it was easier and better to keep up than to fall out and get behind and then have to catch up. This prompted an inquiry of his captain, who said that the man was private Levi Gleason, a Methodist minister, a drafted man, a good soldier and a pleasant good fellow and comrade.

He was called to headquarters one evening soon afterwards, and invited, the regiment having no chaplain, to preach to us at the next convenient opportunity. He excused himself for want of preparation, but finally consented, and on the first Sabbath of rest in camp the regiment assembled at the "church call" at the Colonel's tent. The opening exercises were in the usual form, many of the men joining in singing the familiar hymns; then private Gleason announced his text, "See that ye fall not out by the way," and gave us an earnest, practical discourse, so appropriate and so illustrated by the common experience of his hearers that it "warmed the boys up for good," as one of them expressed it.

Milledgeville, then the capital city of Georgia, was an ancient, aristocratic place with handsomely shaded streets and dwellings, but it wore an air of quiet decadence and lack of enterprise. The legislature had hastily adjourned the day before our arrival, and the Governor had departed with the members. Gen. Sherman occupied the executive mansion with army headquarters, while some of our officers assembled at the capitol and reorganized the legislature, repealed the ordinance of secession and adopted a preamble and resolution declaring the loyalty of the State of Georgia to the Union. All these proceedings being approved by the provisional governor and duly spread upon the journals of the two houses, the improvised legislature adjourned, to meet successively in the capitals of South Carolina, North Carolina and Virginia.

On the 25th of November we crossed the Oconee river, and next day reached Sandersville. On the 27th we crossed the Ogeechee river, and on the 28th arrived at Louisville, where we remained two days awaiting some movements by the other corps. The enemy's cavalry, under Gen. Wheeler, had been very active of late, burning all the bridges ahead of our column and annoying and capturing our foragers whenever they could be taken by surprise. We could pontoon the streams without much delay, but did not want our foraging interfered with; so Kilpatrick was ordered to punish and drive away the offenders, and our (Baird's) division was sent along to support him. Some lively skirmishing occurred during the next three or four days between the opposing cavalry forces, but they kept out of the way of our infantry, generally, and we didn't get much fun out of the campaign. On the 4th we drove the enemy through and beyond Waynesboro, and then turned southeasterly, and on the 5th encamped at Alexander. Now followed several days of unpleasant weather, obstructed roads and slow progress, with continued annoyance and skirmishing with the enemy's cavalry. On the 8th we had quite a brush with them, in which private George Boyson, of Company "K," was mortally wounded. This day we crossed the Ebenezer creek as rear guard, and were closely pressed by the enemy while our bridge was being taken up. On the 10th we destroyed a section of the Charleston and Savannah railroad, including a portion of the trestle bridge at the west bank of the Savannah river. Now we had left behind us the fine agricultural country of central Georgia, abounding in corn, hogs, cattle and sweet potatoes; had also passed through a level section of sandy pine lands, almost destitute of population, improvements or provisions, and found ourselves among the rice plantations of the Savannah river and coast region. The rice crop had been harvested and the threshing and hulling mills were in operation. These were fired by the enemy at our approach, but our cavalry saved one of the threshing mills in the vicinity of our division, the hulling machinery being destroyed. So for six or seven days we had rice in abundance, issued to the troops "with the bark on." We had rice for breakfast, rice for dinner, rice for supper and rice the next day and the next. Rice for the soldiers, for the horses, for the negroes and for the mules, and for everybody. The boys exhausted their ingenuity in contriving various ways of hulling and cooking it, but it was always *rice*, and we got so sick of it that some of us have never eaten any of the stuff since. We were very glad when our regiment was ordered out on the 16th on a foraging expedition, which promised at least a temporary change of diet. We went out in a southwesterly direction and loaded our train with forage; got a few cattle and some miscellaneous provisions, all there was in the country, and returned on the 19th; were shelled by one of the enemy's batteries at a distance on our return, and private Stevens, of Company "H," was wounded. A wide flooded rice field between us and the battery made it inaccessible to us, so we had to leave it behind, much to our regret.

Meanwhile, Fort McAllister had been captured by Hazen's division on the 12th, opening communication with our fleet, and on our return we found 40 days' accumulated mail in our camp and two or three days later, provisions and supplies came in from the fleet by transports; among these supplies nothing was so welcome as the Irish potatoes, of which we had seen none in the past six weeks. On the night of the 20th the enemy evacuated Savannah and some of our forces entered it at daybreak on the 21st. Our brigade, however, encamped in a pleasant field about a mile from the line of defences constructed by the enemy about the city, and our officers and men were permitted to visit the city and explore the country about it. Some of them discovered that the oyster beds below the city had been between the guns of the blockading fleet and the enemy's shore batteries for two years and thus had not been fished. A detail of men with six big army wagons were sent down there and returned on Christmas Eve with several hundred bushels of the big and luscious oysters to enrich our Christmas dinner.

Christmas came on Sunday and Private Gleason preached for us again. About this time a request for his discharge, signed by the Presiding Elder and other clergymen of the Minnesota Conference, addressed to the Secretary of War, was by that authority referred to his regimental commander for his opinion and report thereon. Now, it was refered to Private Gleason for his remarks. They were to the effect that he believed that in his conscription his place and field of duty had been by the Divine Ruler indicated to him, that he had found ample opportunity in it to serve Him and do good to his fellows, and that grateful to his friends for their kind efforts in his behalf, he did not desire his discharge until the war should end. Then the paper was returned to the Secretary of War and, quite unexpectedly to him, Private Gleason was appointed Chaplain of the regiment, an office he filled most acceptably to the final discharge of the regiment.

On the 27th of December the 14th corps passed in review before Gen. Sherman in the city of Savannah. Our regiment was especially complimented by him as it well deserved, and a few days later was ordered into the city, and put in charge of the yard and shops and other property of the Central Railroad. The officers occupied the general office building and the regiment was housed in the great freight warehouse adjoining the yards.

Here, with daily drills and dress parades in the park-like streets, and with guard and patrol duty, we had a pleasant though busy tour of service.

Information was here received of the assignment of two detachments of recruits from Fort Snelling to our regiment, one of which had been forwarded as far as Nashville, and there detained by Gen.

Thomas until after the battles of the 15th and 16th of December, in which our recruits participated, and Maj. C. S. Uline was sent to find and bring them to the regiment. This he did with all possible expedition, but we left Savannah before his return and he joined us later at Goldsboro, N. C. (See Appendix No. 26.)

CHAPTER XIII.

SAVANNAH TO RALEIGH.

On the 23rd of January, 1865, we commenced the "Campaign of the Carolinas," no less famous in history than "The March to the Sea."

Of these campaigns the following general remarks, by way of comparison, may be permitted. The march through Georgia was made in the forty days commencing the 12th of November at Kingston and ending with the evacuation of Savannah on the 21st of December. This was, in that country, the most agreeable and every way the most favorable season of the year for such a campaign. The weather was generally delightful, the roads in good condition, the streams running parallel with our course, were always within their banks and easily forded or bridged, and the bountiful harvest, being just over, there was abundance of provisions and forage on every plantation. The march was moreover a surprise to the enemy, from which he did not recover in time to give us any serious opposition.

The Carolina campaign comprised the sixty-three days ending with the arrival at Goldsboro, March 23rd, including the battle of Bentonville, on the 20th. This was the winter season of cold rains, with occasional snows, and the roads were usually bad; sometimes impassable for loaded wagons and artillery until they had been corduroyed by the troops. The streams were full, often overflowing their banks, and as they crossed our course at right angles, much time and labor had to be spent in bridging them. The enemy had meantime collected, under active commanders, quite a formidable and well organized force, and disputed our crossing at every stream, and harrassed and captured our foragers at every opportunity. The surplus provisions and forage had, moreover, during the winter, been gathered and sent to Lee's army in Virginia or had been consumed on the plantations, and it required active work for a detail of thirty men to gather daily the supplies of food for the regiment. In the Georgia campaign there had been but little bitterness of feeling toward us displayed by the people at home there and but little wanton destruction or waste of property by the soldiers; in the Carolinas, and especially in South Carolina, the bummers had to hunt and fight for everything they got, and they left nothing behind them that they could burn or carry off. In the interest of discipline as well as of humanity the officer in charge of the detail, made daily from our regiment, was always instructed not to burn buildings or abuse the resident people or to take or destroy property not needed for our own use, and it is the writer's belief that his men had but small part in the cruel and wanton devastation that marked the pathway of the army across that state.

But to resume our narrative within its proper limits, our regiment marched out of their comfortable quarters at the Central Railroad depot at 7 A.M. on the 20th, and at 10 o'clock encamped at Cherokee Hill, eight miles out on the Augusta road, by which we had approached the city a month earlier. We left this camp on the 25th, and bridging and crossing one branch of Ebenezer Creek on the 26th and another on the 27th, passing that day through the pretty village of Springfield, we encamped on the 28th near Sister's Ferry on the Savannah river, about forty miles above the city. Here we remained a week while a pontoon bridge was being thrown across the river and a corduroy road built across the wide and overflowed bottom lands on the South Carolina side, and while trains and artillery were being crossed. On the 5th of February we marched over and, encamping three miles from the bridge, waited there while it was being taken up on the 6th; next day we passed through the smouldering ruins of Robertsville and Brighton, which had been burned the day before by our own troops ahead of us. Our course now lay west of north, parallel to and a few miles distant from the Savannah River until the 10th, when we turned a little to the right and, crossing the Salkehatchie River, arrived at Barnwell Court House. Our brigade had the advance to-day, and as we came in sight of the village an order was received from corps headquarters for our regiment to encamp therein and prevent any firing of buildings or any molestation of the inhabitants. As every house in sight of our march from Sister's Ferry had been burned, with no attempt to restrain or prevent the lawless destruction, it seemed that a difficult duty had been assigned to us. Our pace was quickened, and as we entered the village in advance of all other troops, guards were stationed at all the houses and the bummers and stragglers were admonished as they came up to keep in the streets and move on. They were greatly surprised at this unexpected restraint, and some of them were not disposed to submit to it, but no serious resistance was made, and by sunset the village was as quiet and peaceful as could be desired. One commissioned officer who had joined the bummers announced his purpose to burn the town anyhow and "he would like to see the guards that would stop him." He thought better of it, however, and halted and sneaked off before a guard's levelled musket, just in time to save his life. We remained here until noon next day, when, our corps having passed on, we were ordered to follow. Before we were half a mile away the village was on fire in a dozen places, and was no doubt totally destroyed.

On the 12th we reached the Augusta & Charlestown Railroad, twenty-four miles east of Augusta. Here we turned eastward, and spent most of the afternoon in destroying the track and bridges. This work was resumed next morning. In the afternoon we marched about ten miles northerly, to Davis' Mills, on the South Edisto river, our brigade being rear guard of the 14th corps. Next morning, the

14th, we crossed the river and burned the bridge behind us. Then marched seventeen miles to the North Edisto. On the 15th we crossed Congaree creek, at Clark's Mills. The roads were bad and we had considerable work in corduroying the soft places and helping the heavy wagons out of the mud. Next day we crossed Twelve Mile Creek, and passed through the smoking ruins of Lexington Court House. On the 17th we waited in camp all the forenoon, while the troops and trains ahead of us, crossed the Saluda river, which was a wide, swift and muddy stream, and had been bridged by our pontoniers. We marched about 5 P. M. over the swaying bridge and on into the night. The wind was blowing hard and the whole country seemed on fire. Columbia, six miles away, lighted up the eastern sky, and the woods and the fences and buildings and the stacks of straw and forage were everywhere ablaze. Along the road were some "deadening" fields in which the pine trees had been killed by girdling and left to decay standing, while the ground was tilled beneath them. The fire would climb these dead trees, following streaks of turpentine or pitch and running out the great bare limbs, would find the fat pitchy knots and there burst out in flaming torches that seemed to be suspended in the sky with no visible support. In some of the regiments that had encamped in one of these deadenings, some of the men were seriously hurt by the falling of limbs that had been burned off the trees over them Columbia was occupied to-day by the 15th corps, and we hear they made a lively night of it there. On the 18th our march was resumed but was slow and tedious, most of the time being spent in corduroying the bottomless roads and extricating the wagons from the mud holes. At night we encamped near the Broad river, opposite Alston, which was an important railroad junction, about twenty-five miles north-west of Columbia. Next morning, Sunday, we crossed the river and destroyed several miles of railroad track and burned a train of cars and a depot; then attended divine service in camp in the afternoon. On Monday we marched northward to Monticello, and on Tuesday eastward to Winnsboro, on the Columbia & Chester railroad. Wednesday, the 22nd, we tackled the railroad again and dissected four or five miles of it.

Our course for a few days had been through a fine productive country, and forage and provisions had been plentiful. On the 23rd we moved eastward about fifteen miles to the Catawba River at Rocky Mount, where our pontoniers were laying a bridge. The stream was wide and full from the recent rains, and the current rapid and swirly. It required all the available bridge equipment, and moreover was a work of great difficulty to span the river with a safe and adequate structure. The 20th corps had hardly crossed ahead of us when the bridge was broken by driftwood floating down the river. The next three days were spent in replacing it and making and keeping it as secure as possible, while a crew of men in boats were put in the river above it to intercept the drift wood and tow it to the shore. Meantime it rained nearly all the time, and the roads as well as the streams were getting worse. Our troops and trains had, however, been crossing at such times as the bridge seemed safe, and at 7 o'clock on the evening of the 27th our turn as the rear brigade came to cross. We lighted our precarious way with pitch pine torches as we moved down the narrow, winding bottomless road to the west bank, and gingerly walked over the slender, swaying chain of canvass boats, and then up the slippery hill on the eastern shore, where we halted and waited for daylight. We had been delayed here several days, and Sherman, who was ahead with the 20th corps, was getting impatient. The rains continued, but nothing could now make the roads any worse than the 23rd corps had left them after the passage of its trains and artillery. We commenced at daybreak, now cutting a new parallel road through the woods and now corduroying the old one, as one or the other seemed best, and by working hard all day forwarded our train three or four miles while the pontoniers were taking up the bridge. Next day, March 1st, we made 15 miles, encamping near Hanging Rock battleground, where Sumpter and Tarleton met in the Revolutionary War. On the 4th we crossed the line into North Carolina, and on the 5th encamped near the Great Pedee river at Sneadsboro The six days' march between the two rivers, with continuous rain and mud, had been the most uncomfortable and fatiguing of the whole campaign, and we were not sorry to have one pleasant day in camp while the bridge was being thrown across the stream. At intervals we heard explosions down the river, and wondered whether the 15th and 17th corps were having a battle at Cheraw, or, as we afterwards learned, were burning some captured ordnance stores.

On the 17th, the bridge having been completed, we crossed the river at noon, and then the rain commenced again and continued for three days more. Our route lay through the piney country of North Carolina, whose products, as our child's geographies had told us, were pitch, tar, rosin, turpentine and lumber. The bummers, as usual, set fire to everything that would burn, and our division arriving one day at a stream swollen bank full, found its surface covered with flames and the bridge burning. A turpentine factory a little way up the stream was on fire, and several hundred barrels of burning tar and melted rosin had flowed into the water and spread over the full width of the stream, making it impossible to cross or even to approach it. So we bivouacked until the burning stream cooled off enough to permit our reconstruction of the bridge. This incident delayed the division five or six hours, and we had to make it up after we got started again. On the 10th our brigade had the lead of the army, and, as we came in sight of Fayetteville, found the enemy in our front. Our progress was disputed for several miles, without, however, much delaying us, and we entered the city about 11 A. M., driving the enemy's rear guard into and through and beyond it, saving the bridge over Cape Fear river by a lively skirmish and a race for it.

Next day a boat arrived from Wilmington with dispatches for Sherman. Our regiment was detailed for provost guard and made responsible for good order and protection of persons and property of the residents during our occupation of the place. We had a pleasant tour of duty here with good weather and some rest. The old U. S. arsenal which had been in operation for the past four years making ordinance stores for the Confederate army was, by Gen. Sherman's order, destroyed; the buildings razed and the expensive machinery broken up.

On the 15th our regimental commander received orders to burn a large cotton factory and warehouse in the city which had been manufacturing goods for the C. S. army, and this was done, to the infinite sorrow of the throng of girls and other operatives who witnessed it. On the 16th the movement of the army towards Goldsboro commenced, and the laborious mending of roads and boosting of wagons was resumed and continued until we encountered the enemy in force at Bentonville on the 20th. Our brigade was but lightly engaged here, but behaved gallantly, our regiment losing two men wounded. Remaining on the battlefield one day, our march was resumed on the 22nd, and next day we crossed the Neuse river and encamped at Goldsboro. Here we found Gens. Terry and Scofield with the 10th and 23rd corps, all resplendent in new uniforms and well supplied with camp equipage and regulation army rations. Our army, in the sixty-three days of hard campaigning, with no opportunity to draw new clothing or even mend what we wore, had come to that condition when a general change of dress and a chance to wash off the tar smoke was eminently desirable. Moreover, understanding that we were to rest a few days at Goldsboro, our foraging details had been instructed that day to provide as large a supply of miscellaneous provisions as possible, and they had been unusually successful, every regiment having at its head the motley cavalcade of bummers and their equipage well laden with assorted plunder. As we approached the city, orders came to close up the column and prepare to pass in review before Gens. Scofield and Terry, to whom Sherman, Slocum and Howard proposed to exhibit the army of which they were so justly proud. It may be supposed that our own commanders, in thinking of the splendid achievements of the army, had quite forgotten the condition it was now in, and that its appearance as the column passed the reviewing stand was a surprise to them as well as to the distinguished officers invited to review us. At all events the "review" was abruptly discontinued after the first two or three brigades had passed, and we went on to our camps without further ceremony. After a day's rest in camp our regiment was ordered out six miles from Goldsboro to guard and operate a grist mill, in which vocation we acquitted ourselves creditably, as usual. Next day we received a mail, the first since the 5th of February, and supplies of clothing, ammunition and army rations of food were issued to the men. On the 31st a military execution took place in another division of our corps, the troops being paraded under arms to witness the sad ceremony. Without any previous notice, our regiment was carefully and thoroughly inspected on the 1st day of April, by an officer from corps headquarters. He commended everything but the band. He commended this also; with their silver horns and magnificent music, but he reminded the commanding officer that regimental bands had long since been abolished, and he would have to report this one to the corps commander as unauthorized. It had to be explained to him that these men were only the authorized company musicians, and not a band at all, though the appearance might be to the contrary, and he duly verified the explanation by examination of the muster rolls. Then he said that the corps commander (Gen. J. C. Davis) had often observed those men and mistaken them for a band, and suggested that to undeceive him they should play at corps headquarters that afternoon, which they did, and were highly complimented as "company musicians." Let it be here said that this band, since its first organization at Tuscumbia, Ala., in the summer of 1862, had been under the same discipline as the companies had been, always having equal hours of drill and practice, always marching in their places at the head of the regiment, and always ready to play the regiment out of camp and from a halt, and when in camp the dress parade and the concert at retreat were never omitted in good weather.

On the 3rd of April, Maj. Uline rejoined the regiment with 80 recruits from Minnesota, whose names filled up our rolls to the number required to entitle the regiment to a Colonel, so on the same day Lieut. Col. J. W. Bishop, who, nine months before, had been commissioned Colonel, was mustered as such, and Maj. Uline was mustered as Lieutenant Colonel, and Capt. John Moulton as Major. Next day our division was reviewed by Gen. Scofield, who had for a time commanded the division in which it was included at Triune, Tenn., in the spring of 1863. He personally congratulated the Colonel on his new rank and on the splendid appearance of his regiment. On the 9th Sergt. Kelsey reported with 59 more recruits which had been forwarded from Minnesota in November, '64, and had spent the winter in Gen. Thomas' command at Nashville, Tenn. On the 10th of April our army was again in motion, towards Raleigh, our brigade leading the army of Georgia twelve miles to Springfield, driving the enemy before us all day. They fired the bridge over Neuse river as they crossed it, and as it had been well prepared with tar and pitch for burning, we were unable to save it. Next morning we received the news of the surrender of Lee's army, and the camps resounded with cheers. Johnston's army was, however, yet before us, and we went for him again, moving him back towards Raleigh twelve miles more, to Clayton. Next day we had a skirmish fight all the way to Raleigh, fifteen miles, arriving there at noon. Our regiment was at once placed in charge of the state insane asylum there, and encamped in the ample grounds, placing a chain of guards about it to keep away the bummers, who were ready to turn out the inmates, sane or insane, without discrimination or formality.

After a day's rest here we marched again on the 15th six miles to Holly Springs and next day six miles further toward Durham Station. We remained in this vicinity during the ten days occupied in the first, and the final negotiations for the surrender of Johnston's army, which took place at Durham on the 26th, and of which we were formally informed on the 27th.

We cannot here discuss the terms of capitulation first offered to Sherman and accepted by Johnston and disapproved at Washington, nor the trouble among high officers that grew out of them. It may perhaps be said that Sherman with his splendid army at his back and his old enemy before him, starved, demoralized and at his mercy, was too generous, but what can be said in extenuation of the treatment accorded to Sherman by the Secretary of War and by Halleck, whose puerile attempt to belittle Sherman and magnify himself is an illustration of mean selfishness in high authority that, were it not in the authentic record over his own signature, would hardly be credited.

But now the campaign was over without serious bloodshed and our rejoicing was unbounded. The paroling of the surrendered men was assigned to Gen. Schofield and we returned by easy marches to the vicinity of Raleigh, encamping Saturday, the 29th, at Page's Station, a short distance west of the city.

CHAPTER XIV.

RICHMOND, WASHINGTON AND HOME.

With the surrender of Johnston's army the war, so far as we were concerned, was substantially over, and we all knew that a few weeks, more or less, would emancipate us from the restraints of military service and restore us to the peaceful avocations of civil life.

Orders were received on Sunday, the 30th of April, to "prepare for a comfortable and leisurely march to Richmond." The troops were to carry only ten rounds of cartridges, all surplus stores, ammunition and supplies being turned in for storage and we were notified that we would be expected at Richmond about the 10th of May, which would make our march about 16 miles a day. This, for a veteran army homeward bound, with good roads, good weather and no enemy in the way, was easy enough. The march was to commence on Monday, the 1st of May, but on Sunday morning, under the pretence of changing the troops to more eligible camps, the Fourteenth corps was led out about 16 miles and encamped at 3 P. M. The remainder of the afternoon was spent in mustering the men and preparing the pay rolls (which had to be done on the last day of every second month) to the exclusion of divine service. The Fourteenth and Twentieth corps were to march on parallel roads and there were suggestions that a racing match had been arranged between the corps commanders, which, if true, was foolish, cruel and unjustifiable, and if it was not true, the hard marching of the next six days has never been reasonably explained, to our knowledge.

On the 1st of May the reveille sounded long before daylight, and we marched at 5 o'clock, crossing Neuse and Tar rivers and encamping at 6 P. M., after a march of twenty-four miles. On the 2nd we made twenty-two miles, and on the 3rd, with a delay of five hours in bridging and crossing Roanoke river at Taylor's Ferry, we marched sixteen miles and encamped near Boydton, Virginia. On the 4th we marched again at 5 o'clock A. M., making twenty-two miles. On the 5th the march was urged all day long and twenty-eight miles were covered, and on Saturday, the 6th, twenty-four miles. On Sunday, the 7th, twenty miles brought our division within a mile of the James river at Richmond, and here orders were received from Maj. Gen. H. W. Halleck, commanding the department of the James, directing the approaching troops to encamp at least six miles south of the city and forbidding any officer or soldier from Sherman's army to enter it unless he had a written pass from his corps commander. Gen. Sherman, not expecting our arrival so soon, was absent, and in partial and reluctant compliance with these orders, the weary troops retraced their steps some two or three miles and went into camp.

In the next two days a good many of Sherman's officers and soldiers did visit the city without the required written pass, greatly to the vexation of the provost guards, who were expected to prevent their crossing the river and to arrest and imprison all who might be found in the city without proper authority.

On the 9th, Sherman still being absent, orders from "Headquarters Department of the James" were received and published to our army announcing a grand review of the Fourteenth army corps in Richmond on the 10th by the "Major General commanding the Department." This order prescribed with infinite detail the line of march by which the corps was to be brought into the august presence of the department commander, the formation of the troops in the column and the position in which the arms were to be carried in passing the several streets, and especially the honors to be paid the reviewing officer. All baggage wagons and camp followers and irregulars of every sort were to be rigorously excluded from the column, and the soldiers and their arms and equipments were to be in the highest degree in military order and condition. Gen. Sherman arrived late that night, but in time to announce to the troops before daybreak that the proposed review would not take place as arranged.

Our arrival had been several days earlier than had been expected, and he now ordered the quartermasters and paymasters, who were on the way to meet us, back to Washington and decided to march his army through to the Potomac at once. He seemed to think that we had been sufficiently entertained and refreshed already in the "Department of the James."

On the 10th our marching orders were received and next day the Fourteenth and Twentieth army corps marched through the city in their free-and-easy "route step," paying no honors to anybody.

Since Johnston's surrender no foraging on the country had been done, and the bummers had been gradually reduced to the ranks and to discipline and order, but on this day's march they were revived and displayed in unusual exuberance of style, spirit and equipment. The provost guards who lined the streets looked on them in wondering amazement, but the Commander of the Department of the James was nowhere visible to the naked eye. We marched twenty-three miles that day, crossing Chickahominy river, and in the thirteen miles next day passed through Hanover Court House and crossed Panumkey river. On the 13th we crossed the Richmond & Gordonville Railroad at Chesterfield and after a morning's march of twelve miles halted at noon at Childsburg, then we marched four miles northwesterly and encamped.

On the 14th we marched twenty miles, encamping near Danielsville, and on the 15th, after passing through Verdiersville we crossed the Rapidan at Racoon Ford, nineteen miles. On the 16th we made eighteen miles, crossing the Rappahannock at Kelly's Ford and next day marched eighteen miles and encamped at Bristoe Station on the Orange & Alexandria Railroad. We were now traversing historic ground and were much interested in noting places whose names were so familiar in association with the movements of the army of the Potomac. On the 18th we passed Manassas Junction, the Bull Run battle field, and Centreville in a march of twenty miles, and on the 19th moved our camp about six miles to Alexandria. Here, on the 20th, seventy-two more recruits from Minnesota joined the regiment and were distributed to companies, and the commissaries, quartermasters and paymasters supplied our needs in their respective departments.

Orders were received announcing the Grand Final Review in Washington of the two great representative armies, that of the Army of the Potomac on the 23rd and of Sherman's Army on the 24th of May, and a day or two was given for rest and preparation. Our regiment was in splendid condition and well armed and equipped in every particular. We numbered about 300 veterans of nearly four years' service, and 400 recruits of one year or less, but these had been so well mingled with and instructed by the veterans that there was little apparent difference in appearance or efficiency. There were few, if any, other regiments in our corps so strong as ours—many of them numbered less than 300 men, the policy in most of the states having been to organize new regiments rather than to fill up the old ones. Our ten companies, under arms, averaged about thirty-two files front and to condense the marching column for the review the smaller regiments were formed into eight or six and some of them into four companies of about that size.

The Fifteenth, Seventeenth and Twentieth corps crossed Long Bridge during the night of the 23rd and bivouacked in the streets about the Capitol to be in readiness to commence the march at the appointed hour. The morning of Wednesday, the 24th, was clear and sunny. Taking an early breakfast in our own camp, our Fourteenth corps was in motion at 7 o'clock and after a march of eight miles stacked arms in the vicinity of the Capitol at 10 o'clock. The review march had already commenced, but there were sixty-five thousand men in the column, which marching briskly consumed six and a half hours in passing the reviewing stand, so our time to march out into Pennsylvania avenue did not come until afternoon.

Probably no more magnificent military display was ever seen than the one that greeted our eyes as we marched around the Capitol and looked down the long, straight, broad avenue, filled from curb to curb with marching troops, the gay uniforms and glistening muskets and the unfolded colors all swaying with the rythm of the music as the regiments with regular, steady step, moved on. At the great Treasury building the column wheeled by companies to the right and then presently to the left, and then the arms were smartly brought to the "carry" for the "march past" the President and the high officers of the army and of the government standing with him. Officers saluted respectfully as they passed the stand, and when the rear company of a regiment had cleared the White House grounds, the arms were "right shouldered" and the route step resumed. No halt for rest was permitted, as the march of the column in the avenue must not be checked or obstructed by the troops ahead of it, so we tramped on through Georgetown and across the Acqueduct bridge into Virginia before we had an opportunity to file out of the road and stack arms and take breath. When we got back to our camps at 7 o'clock we had marched twenty miles, and were pretty thoroughly tired. Probably the reviewing officers, who stood for several consecutive hours looking at the passing troops, were also tired, but they did not, as we did, have to march with a soldier's load ten miles to get there and then ten miles to supper.

On the day after the review our corps left the old bivouac at Alexandria and moved about ten miles to find a fresher and cleaner camping ground, about three miles north of Washington. Here the officers and men were freely given opportunity to visit the city, and, with pleasant weather and plentiful rations, the time passed rapidly and without many events worthy of notation here. Our old commander, George H. Thomas, visited our camp on the 23rd of June, and was enthusiastically received by our regiment and others that had served with him and under him, in the West.

On the 3rd he reviewed our division, which had been his original command in 1861, and under his direction had fought and won the battle of Mill Springs.

On the 6th of June our (third) division (14th army corps) was reorganized; and Col. J. W. Bishop was formally assigned to command the first brigade, now consisting of the 2nd Minnesota, 18th Kentucky, 31st Ohio, 101st Indiana and 23rd Missouri regiments, and on the 9th he assumed command of the division, Gen. Baird having taken leave of absence. On the 13th of June his commission as Brigadier General by Brevet, dated

April 9th, 1865, was received and was duly announced to the regiment. (*See appendix No. 28.*) In the evening the officers and men of the regiment, with the band, came to division headquarters *en masse* to present their congratulations. Some twenty-five years later the writer learned that this appointment had been recommended by his corps and army commanders from Savannah in January, 1865, and, the commission not having arrived, the recommendation was renewed in May. (*See appendix No. 29.*)

On the 14th orders were received to move the division by rail to Parkersburg, on the Ohio river, and thence by steamers to Louisville, Ky., and the first brigade was forwarded in the afternoon of the same day, the remainder of the division following next morning. The troops travelled in open coal cars, which at the time were the only cars to be had for them, and they would have been comfortable enough in fine weather, but it rained all the first night on the road, drenching the men, and with the coal dust making their beds decidedly dirty and uncomfortable. Division headquarters left Washington by passenger train in the evening of the 15th, and, passing the troops on the road, arrived at Cumberland in time next morning to have hot coffee supplied to all the troop trains as they came along, which was gratefully appreciated by the tired and hungry men. The division arrived at Parkersburg on the 17th, and next day, Sunday the 18th, embarked on a fleet of steamers for the trip down the Ohio river. We had a most delightful voyage, passing Cincinnati at 6 P. M. of

Monday, arrived at Louisville Tuesday morning, the 20th, and, marching out on the Bardstown pike, encamped about four miles south of the city. Here the next twenty days were passed in waiting the decision of the war department as to our final discharge. Some of the troops were being sent to Texas and to other Southern states, and while we knew that the larger part of the army would be soon discharged, we could not know that we might not be elected to remain in the service indefinitely. But orders came at last for our muster out, and on the 10th of July the rolls were all ready, and the final inspection, muster and parade was made. Orders relieving all detached duty men had been received, and our camp and garrison equipage were turned over to the Quartermaster.

The corps commander issued his farewell orders, directing the regiment to proceed to Fort Snelling, Minnesota, for final discharge, and accompanied them with a complimentary letter. (*Appendix Nos. 30, 31 and 32.*)

The officers of the regiment called on Gen. Baird, our division commander, in the evening, and received his parting congratulations and commendations. He had, as our division commander since October, 1863, won the hearty respect and good will of all under his command, and, with all our eagerness to be released from military duty, there was mingled much of regret at the breaking up of all our well established and agreeable relations as soldiers.

Next morning, the 11th, we marched out of our camps at 6 o'clock, leaving the tents all standing, and a few minutes later halted at corps headquarters, where Gen. J. C. Davis, the corps commander, made us a brief but feeling address, and said good-by; then the march was resumed to Louisville; there we crossed the Ohio river, and at 10 o'clock we left Jeffersonville by train for Chicago, where on arrival at 6 P. M. next day the regiment was quartered in the Soldiers' Rest. Early on the 13th we marched through the city and took the train for La Crosse by way of Watertown, Wis. Reaching La Crosse at 2 A. M. on the 14th, we immediately went on board the steamer McLellan for St. Paul.

At Winona at 8 o'clock a crowd of people were at the levee to greet us, and the captain kindly consented to hold the boat there long enough to permit us to go ashore for a parade march. The men were in high spirits, and with our splendid band and full ranks the regiment marched through the broad, level streets for an hour or more and then stacked arms to enable the men to exchange greetings and congratulations with the citizens and with their friends, many of whom had come from interior counties to see us. Winona had hospitably entertained us on several occasions, and we all gratefully remembered it.

Next morning, the 15th, we landed at the lower levee at St. Paul. The city seemed to be having a general holiday, and crowds of people were on the bank to welcome us, with bands of music and salvos of artillery, and a parade of the fire department and other organizations. Col. John T. Averill, of the 6th Minnesota regiment, marshaled the grand procession, and under its escort we marched in columns of platoons up Third street to Wabasha, and by that street to the Capitol grounds, where we were received by Hon. John S. Prince, then Mayor of the city, and Hon. Stephen Miller, then Governor of the state, in appropriate addresses of welcome. Then we were invited to a bountiful collation which the ladies had spread for us in the Capitol building and which they personally served to the hungry soldiers with gracious words and kind attentions.

All this over, our march was resumed to the upper levee, where we re-embarked for Fort Snelling. About 5 o'clock P. M. we were encamped on the parade ground at that historic post, where four years before we had been mustered into the service. Here we were obliged to wait several days for our final payment. Our camp was enlivened with visiting friends during the day, and throngs of people came out every evening from St. Paul and from Minneapolis to attend our dress parades. At the close of the last parade of the regiment, Wednesday evening, July 19th, a brief farewell address was made to the regiment by the Colonel. The next day, July 20th, the final payment was made, the men received their individual discharges, and the "Second Regiment of Minnesota Veteran Volunteer Infantry" ceased to exist. The men dispersed to their homes with a loyal pride in the record made by the regiment, with a warm and steadfast friendship for each other as comrades, and with the satisfaction that comes only from duty well performed. "May God bless and prosper them, every one!" was the sincere prayer of the Commander as the men affectionately bade him good-by on that bright summer afternoon, and now, after twenty-five years have intervened with varied experiences of sadness and of happiness to us all, he closes the record with the same "God bless and prosper you, comrades, every one!"

CHAPTER XV.

CONCLUDING REMARKS.

The war through which this narrative has taken us ended nearly twenty-five years ago.

A generation of young men born since our muster out, are now voters and of full age for military service. Many of them are enrolled as members of the National Guard in the several states and doubtless would be as prompt and ready as their fathers were, to take the field for the National defense if the country required their services. And probably in any future war of like duration the deplorable waste and sacrifice of soldiers' lives and health through ignorance and incompetence of officers and men under unaccustomed circumstances, would be repeated. Some things in war have to be personally learned by experience, and a brief relation of some of these things will interest old comrades as a reminiscence, if it does not meet the notice of any who might derive instruction from it.

At the President's call our companies were assembled and recruited at their several local stations, and when ready were ordered to the general rendezvous at Fort Snelling to be mustered into the United States service and to be organized into regiments. The men and officers of each company were mutual acquaintances and friends, while they were strangers to those of other companies, and this with other obvious causes begot and promoted a spirit of company pride, which, if they had been brought together for a few days' encampment and exercise, or for a short period of service within the state, would not be objectionable, perhaps indeed would be desirable as a stimulus for each to do its best. The rules of promotion were established on this line at the beginning, under which all vacant commissions occurring in any company were to be filled by promotion from its own ranks.

When, however, the regiment left the state and took its place among the hundreds of other regiments in the Grand Army of the United States this company feeling gave place in great degree to the larger one of pride and comradeship in the regiment, and the propriety of the regimental rule of promotion, which was adopted and announced by the Governor in 1863, became manifest. Under this rule the vacant commission in any company was to be filled by the senior of the next lower grade in the regiment, promotions to the grade of Second Lieutenant being made within the company.

Details of entire companies for guard and picket and fatigue duty, which were at first the rule, gradually were superseded by details of officers and men from all the companies, which promoted better acquaintance and better discipline, and better distributed the duty with its casualties and hardships throughout the regiment.

So the regiment came to be in large degree the unit of command and administration and maneuver, in which all the officers and men were personally known to and interested as comrades in each other, while the company was the family of more intimate and brotherly relations among the men and more immediate and personal care and command by the officers; and the regiment and the company were thus better and more efficiently handled.

At the beginning it was a favorite scheme to brigade together regiments from the same state, to be called the Vermont brigade or the Wisconsin brigade, etc., but this was soon discontinued as unwise and the better plan of mingling the regiments from the various states together was adopted, thus, in organizing a National Army, ignoring state lines. Certain influences effected and maintained the isolation of the Regular troops in separate brigades and when practicable in separate divisions, but this practice was even more objectionable than the separate brigading of state regiments. If a regular regiment was in any way superior to the volunteers, why should not the latter have the advantage of association with it. If it be suggested that the regulars might learn of volunteers, why should they not have the opportunity?

One of the first things the new soldier had to learn was how intelligently and properly to take care of himself. Many of them were mere children in this respect. Accustomed to the comforts and conveniences of life under different conditions, he lacked the provident forethought, and the knack of getting the best out of present circumstances, which became a habit with the veteran, and was therefore continually suffering for want of something which he might have had. Ordered out suddenly on a hard march his already worn out shoes gave out the first day. When night came on cold or stormy his overcoat or blanket had been thrown away to lighten his load on the march. If the trains were mired several miles back in the road our recruit had no food or cooking utensils, though he had received three days rations that very morning. If he got overheated on the march or at drill he would drink a pint of cold spring water at a gulp and become a candidate for hospital treatment directly. If he could sneak out of the column on the road he laid down in the fence corner and took a nap, then if he were not picked up by the enemy he had to march alone and weary far into the night to rejoin his company. If he got sick he got homesick also and lost his heart and hope and died.

Then the officers from General to Captain were often as inexperienced as the men, and indifferent to the comfort and care of their troops. Few of them knew the weight of a knapsack, haversack, canteen, gun and "forty rounds," and the marches were conducted without any intelligent judgment as to economizing the strength of the troops, and the camps were not selected with due regard to convenience and rest. All these things were greatly improved with experience. Within the first year of service in the South our regiment lost from deaths and discharges resulting from wounds in action less than two per cent, but in the same time lost from deaths and discharges for disability resulting from diseases and hardships, over twenty per cent.

Yet the same regiment made the "Campaign of the Carolinas" three years later, in mid-winter, marching 480 miles, foraging on the country chiefly for its rations, with no tents except those carried on the men's backs, and with one half of its men recruits of only a few months' service (well mingled with and instructed by the veterans, however) and arrived at Goldsboro with a total temporary loss from its effective present force of only three per cent. Such a record was not, in this campaign, reached by many regiments, but anything approaching it in the first year of the war would have been quite impossible for any, in the then inexperience of officers and men.

As the war went on, officers learned to require and men to conform to many things in the ways of regulation and discipline that could not be applied and enforced with new troops It came to be understood that somewhere in all the months of weary marching, maneuvering and campaigning, there was to come an hour of actual battle, when the victory must be won by the army that could outfight the other. Failing in this emergency, all else was failure.

To bring a regiment properly and effectively into battle it must have several qualities, only to be developed by long and persistent attention to details, which at times grow tiresome and seem to be arbitrary and unnecessary.

At the crucial hour the regiment must be *present* in full strength and must have its cartridge boxes full—it must be *coherent*, not to be broken up and scattered by something or anything that may happen to it—and it must be *manageable* under all circumstances. Wanting any of these qualities, it is simply a crowd of men of which nothing can be predicted with certainty except confusion and defeat.

As these things came to be realized, some rules were adopted and persistently enforced in our regiment, through a season of reluctance and grumbling, until they came to be habitually and cheerfully observed. One of these was that there should be no straggling on the march, and no wandering from camp without permission. To this end, while in camp the men must be accounted for by the company commanders at the several roll calls, and, if the camp was for more than a day or two, exercises were had, both to require the presence of officers and men, and to promote the efficiency, steadiness and manageability of the regiment. While on the march, men were forbidden to leave the column except with permission in case of necessity. At every halt for rest arms were stacked and absentees, if any, were noted and accounted for, or reported. Relieved of his musket, the tired soldier got his rest with his comrades, and the march was always resumed with music by the band, whose members were also required to keep their places at the head of the regiment. When we encamped for the night our men were always on hand for supper and a full night's rest, or for any duty required.

In the "March to the Sea" we lost not a single man from straggling or capture, while a good many were so lost from other regiments.

Our cartridge boxes were frequently inspected and kept full. Forty rounds of .58 calibre is no light load, but the regiments whose men were allowed to waste or throw them away at their pleasure, often got into disgrace when suddenly called on for duty with empty boxes.

The men themselves came to take pride in being always present and ready, and the records made by the regiment successively at Chicamauga, Mission Ridge, the Veteran Furlough, the March to the Sea and the Carolina Campaign, abundantly justifies the preparation and discipline through which they were achieved.

At the beginning thirteen six-mule wagons were allowed for the transportation of each regiment, one for headquarters' tents, office and baggage, one for quartermaster stores, one for the hospital outfit, and one for the tents and baggage of each company. At this rate the wagons occupied as much space in the road as the regiment did, and when an army corps marched with its brigade, division and corps supplies and ammunition trains, in addition to the regimental wagons, the trains quite overwhelmed the troops.

So in the spring of 1863, when the "pup tents" were issued, the regimental trains were reduced to three wagons, and the other trains were also reduced, though in a less proportion.

This, in anticipation, seemed to be a great hardship, but it proved a positive advantage to the troops. The men now carried what they needed and, arriving at camp, their comfort did not depend on the wagons coming in (as they often did not), and the roads being less encumbered with trains, the troops made their marches easier and quicker.

Most of the regimental bands that went out with the troops disappeared during the first year; they were usually good musicians, but poor soldiers, and, discouraged by the rough ways of war, neglected by the officers who should have looked after them, and despised by the men generally, they were mustered out as expensive supernumararies.

Later on, in our regiment, the company musicians were organized into a band, of which we were justly very proud, and similar action was perhaps taken in other regiments. A good band, always present for duty, even in battle, where they should care for the wounded, is a very important part of a regiment, worth all it costs the government in money or the Commander in care for its discipline and instruction.

Early in the war issues were made to the regiments of axes and shovels for repairing roads, constructing rifle pits and other works of fortification, etc. They were habitually carried in the trains until the company wagons were taken away, but as the trains were usually in the rear and the tools in the bottoms of the wagons, they were seldom available when most needed, and seldom in order for use when within reach. Later the orders were that the men should *carry* these tools in addition to their regular loads. Under these orders the tools were invariably "lost" within the first two or three days, and when suddenly they were wanted in some emergency, the temper of the general officer was also lost, to the great discomfort of subordinates.

In our regiment, after some experience of this kind, a Lieutenant, Sergeant and Corporal, and two privates from each company were selected and called the "pioneers." They were all strong, active and skillful men, were armed only with army revolvers in the belt, and each of the twenty men carried an ax and two shovels. They camped and messed with their companies, but marched at the head of the regiment, always ready for any job in their line. They were inspected as carefully as were their comrades, and their axes were as keen and their shovels as bright as good care could keep them. On the march or in camp the "pioneer call" by the bugler brought this corps promptly to headquarters duly equipped, and at a second call four more men from each company, leaving their guns with their comrades, joined the pioneers, and it was a tough job that was not soon disposed of by the sixty men.

This corps and their effective work attracted considerable attention, and the commander of the 14th corps, in more than one important emergency, witnessed and warmly commended their skill and prompt readiness.

The matter of recruiting and keeping full the regiments in the field has been already alluded to in the narrative, but it deserves perhaps further notice.

The continued call for men in the later years of the war no doubt fully taxed the Governors of the several states. To fill the existing regiments required only individual enlistments, but they had ceased to be spontaneous as they had been in the beginning, and it was much easier to raise a new regiment, with the active assistance of men who expected to be commissioned in it, than to enlist the same number of men for the regiments already at the front.

Experienced officers could not usually be called home from the field to recruit new companies or regiments, and so it often happened that a new regiment of a thousand men, with officers of little or no experience, arrived at the front. The War Department had decreed that, when an old regiment had less than the standard strength, a vacant Coloneley should not be filled, and so in some of the brigades there were no Colonels in any of the regiments, and the brigade itself was commanded by a Lieutenant Colonel, fully competent after three years experience, to command it.

To assign the new regiment to such a brigade would not only weaken it by the large addition of raw and unwieldy material, but would place the new Colonel at once in command of it, which might in the presence of the enemy result in disaster.

So the new regiment was detached to some post or other duty, where, as in several instances happened, John Morgan or some other enterprising

Confederate commander would capture the post, regiment, new guns and all.

In Minnesota the practice was to appoint officers from the older regiments to command the later ones, and more effort was made to recruit the old ones than in some other states.

It is a common mistake to think and speak of the old soldiers as a pitiable lot of physical wrecks whose disability originated in the military service. This is far from the truth. A good many men undoubtedly suffer from such disabilities so incurred, but many of the survivors of the war are indebted to their military service not only for improved physical condition, but for such regulation, education and development of mind and character as have largely contributed to their success in civil life, and no class of men have in the past twenty-five years been more generally successful than the old soldiers. The four years training in habits of patience, courage, self reliance and persistence have given them qualities which count in their whole after life as no small recompense for the hardships and exposure of their army service.

The veterans who survived the war are now old men, yet they are generally, I think, in better physical condition than the average of other men of equal age. A soldier's life is, or should be, temperate, and restrained in respect to many vicious practices and with due care of himself in later years as in the service, the old soldier should be entitled to a comfortable passage down the evening tide of his life as he approaches and enters the Great Beyond.

APPENDIX.

[No. 1.]

ADJUTANT GENERAL'S OFFICE.
ST. PAUL, April 17th, 1861.

CAPT. J. W. BISHOP, Chatfield.

SIR:— With this find three copies of Governor's proclamation and order relative thereto. Will you please get your company together upon receipt of this and report to me as to what course they will take as soon thereafter as possible. I hope to hear from you soon.

Yours respectfully,
WM. H. ACKER, Adjutant General.

[No. 2.]

TELEGRAM.

ST. PAUL, April 22nd, 1861.

J. W. BISHOP, Chatfield, Minn.,
(Care of John Ball, Winona.)

Fill up at once and drill. Your company is accepted and under state pay. Await marching orders. I write by mail.

IGNATIUS DONNELLY, Governor, *ad interim*.

[No. 3.]

EXECUTIVE OFFICE,
ST. PAUL, April 22nd, 1861.

CAPT. J. W. BISHOP, Chatfield, Minn.

Your company is accepted. I have telegraphed you to-day. You must fill up your ranks *at once* and be ready to march to St. Paul upon receipt of order from Adjutant General which will probably be delivered by a special agent.

Very truly and respectfully,
IGNATIUS DONNELLY.

[No. 4.]

ADJUTANT GENERAL'S OFFICE,
St. Paul, Minn., April 26th, 1861.

Capt. J. W. Bishop.

Sir:— You are hereby ordered and required to deliver to the bearer, Wm. H. Shelly, Esq., fifty-nine rifle muskets, delivered to Company "A," 3rd regiment, M. V. M. at the date of its organization, and the accoutrements accompanying the same, for the equipment of the regiment now forming.

John B. Sanborn, Adjutant General.

Chatfield, April 29th, 1861.

I have this morning received from Capt. J. W. Bishop the above orders except swords.

Wm. H. Shelly.

[No. 5.]

Chatfield, May 4th, 1861.

To John B. Sanborn, Adjutant General, etc.

Sir:— I am authorized to tender to you the "Chatfield Guards," eighty men, as unconditional volunteers in the service of the State or of the Federal government, to notify you that they are ready for immediate service and will hold themselves thus in readiness, and to request that this tender be placed on file in your office, and that the "Chatfield Guards" may retain their position at the head of the list of companies already tendered and which were not accepted for the first regiment mustered in response to the call of the President.   Very respectfully yours, etc.,

J. W. Bishop, Captain Chatfield Guards.

[No. 6.]

Chatfield, June 7th, 1861.

John B. Sanborn, Adjutant General.

Sir:— Hearing that the arms and equipments, ordered by Governor Ramsey for the State, have been received at St. Paul, I venture to express the hope that my requisition for sixty stand of arms, with equipments and ammunition, for the "Chatfield Guards" may be filled and forwarded at once.

The "Guards" have sent for uniforms at their own expense and all of the members who reside in this immediate vicinity meet for drill every evening at 6:30 o'clock and on Saturday afternoons. It would add materially to the interest and profit of our drill to have the arms and ammunition and the boys are getting a little impatient at the long delay in sending them.

A tender of our company for any honorable service is on file in your office and the "Guards" will, until the close of the war, hold themselves always at the "ready."

Yours truly,
J. W. BISHOP, Captain "Chatfield Guards."

[No. 7.]

(Adjutant General's report for 1861, page 237.)

GENERAL HEADQUARTERS,
STATE OF MINNESOTA.
ADJUTANT GENERAL'S OFFICE,
ST. PAUL, June 26th, 1861.

CAPT. BISHOP, Second Regiment Minnesota Volunteers.

You will take command of the post of Fort Snelling forthwith and so continue until further orders; and you are hereby announced as such commander and will be obeyed and respected accordingly.

By order of the Commander in Chief,
JOHN B. SANBORN, Adjutant General.

[No. 8.]

CAPTURED FLAGS.

(War of the Rebellion, official records, Series 1, Vol. 7, page 82.)

HEADQUARTERS 1ST DIVISION,
DEPARTMENT OF THE OHIO.
SOMERSET, KY., February 3rd, 1861.

BRIG. GENL. D. C. BUELL,

Commanding Department of the Ohio, Louisville, Ky.

GENERAL:—I have the honor to forward to you by Captain Davidson, 10th Kentucky volunteers, six Rebel flags;

one captured on the battle field by the 2nd Minnesota regiment, the others taken in the intrenchments by officers and men of the other regiments. Col. Kise reports that his men captured three stands of colors, but none have been sent to these headquarters. I have ordered him to turn them in, and will forward them as soon as received. In the box with the colors is the regimental order book of the 15th Mississippi rifles, and a book of copies of all Gen. Zollicoffer's orders from the organization of the brigade until a few days before the battle. I am, General, very respectfully,

Your obedient servant,
GEO. H. THOMAS,
Brigadier General, U. S. Volunteers, commanding.

[No. 9.]

Report of Col. H. P. Van Cleve, commanding reg't.

(War of the Rebellion, official reports, Series 1, Vol. 7, page 95.)

HEADQUARTERS 2ND REGIMENT,
MINNESOTA VOLUNTEERS.
CAMP HAMILTON, KY., January 22nd, 1862.

SIR:—I have the honor herewith to submit my report of the part taken by the 2nd Minnesota regiment in the action of the Cumberland on the 19th inst:

About seven o'clock on the morning of that day, and before breakfast I was informed by Col. Manson, of the 10th Indiana commanding the 2nd brigade of our division, that the enemy was advancing in force and that he was holding them in check, and that it was the order of Gen. Thomas that I should form my regiment and march immediately to the scene of action. Within ten minutes we had left our camp and were marching toward the enemy. Arriving at Logan's field, by your order, we halted in line of battle, supporting Standart's battery, which was returning the fire of the enemy's guns, whose balls and shells were falling near us. As soon as the 9th Ohio came up and had taken its position on our right we continued our march, and after proceeding about half a mile we came upon the enemy, who were posted behind a fence along the road, beyond which there was an open field broken by ravines. The enemy, opening upon us, a galling fire fought desperately, and a hand-to-hand fight ensued, which lasted about thirty minutes.

The enemy having met with so warm a reception in front, and also having been flanked on their left by the 9th Ohio, and on their right by a portion of our left, who, by their well directed fire drove them from behind their hiding places, gave way, leaving a large number of their dead and wounded on the field. We joined in the pursuit which continued till near sunset, when we arrived within a mile of their intrenchments, where we rested on our arms during the night. The next morning we marched into their works which we found deserted. The enemy had crossed the Cumberland.

Six hundred of my regiment were in the engagement, twelve of whom were killed and thirty-three wounded.

I am well satisfied with the conduct of my entire command during the severe and close engagement in which they took part. Where all behaved so well I have no desire to make individual distinction.

Very respectfully, your obedient servant,
H. P. VAN CLEVE,
Colonel commanding 2nd Minnesota Volunteers.

[No. 10.]

BATTLE OF MILL SPRINGS.

List of killed and wounded in 2nd Minn.
(Official files, Adjutant General's office, state of Minnesota.)

KILLED.

Names.	Rank and Co.
H. C. Reynolds	Private B
Milo Crumb	Private B
Wm. H. H. Morrow	Private D
Fred Bohmbach	Private G
John B. Cooper	Private B
Andrew Dresco	Private B
H. R. Thompson	Private E
Gustave Rommel	Private G
Fred Stomshorn	Private G
Jacob Warner	Private G
Sam. H. Parker	Private I
Frank Schneider	Private I

WOUNDED.

Names.	Rank and Co.
Wm. Markham	Capt. B
Tenbrock Stout	2nd Lieut. I
Ed. Cooper	Corp'l B
W. C. Smith	Private B
Ira G. Walden	Private B
John Etzel	Private B
Cornelius White	Private B
J. B. Chamber	Private B
John Mabold	Private E
J. R. Brown	Private E

WOUNDED—CONTINUED.

Names.	Rank and Co.
O. P. Renne	Private E
Anton Morgenstern	Serg'nt G
Frank Kiefer	Private G
Chas. Schultz	Private G
Chas. Yanke	Private G
Henry H. Hammen	Private G
Wm. Kemper	Private G
Geo. Dehnning	Private G
Henry Clinton	Private I
Thos. McDonough	1st Sgt. K
F. V. Hotchkiss	Corp'l K
Alex. Grant	Corp'l K
J. B. Pomeroy	Corp'l K
John Benson	Private K
Henry F. Cook	Private K
Alex. Partman	Private K
W. K. Haskins	Private K
John Smith	Private K
P. S. Barnett	Private K
Thos. Johnson	Private K
G. Plowman	Private K
C. F. Westland	Private K

(No. 11.)

Report of Col. Robert L. McCook, Commanding Brigade.

(War of Rebellion, Official Records, Series 1, Vol. 7, page 93).

HEADQUARTERS 3RD BRIGADE, 1ST DIVISION,
DEPARTMENT OF THE OHIO.
SOMERSET, January 27th, 1862.

SIR:—I have the honor respectfully to submit the following report of the part which my Brigade took in the battle of the Cumberland, on the 9th inst.

Shortly after seven A. M., Col. Manson informed me that the enemy had driven in his pickets and were approaching in force. That portion of the brigade with me, the 9th Ohio and 2nd Minnesota Regiments, were formed and marched to a point near the junction of the Mill Springs and Cumberland roads, and immediately in the rear of Wetmore's battery, the 9th Ohio on the right and the 2nd Minnesota on the left of the Mill Springs road. From this point I ordered a company of the 9th Ohio to skirmish the woods on the right to prevent any flank movement of the enemy. Shortly after this, Col. Manson, commanding the 2nd brigade, informed me in person that the enemy were in force and in position on the top of the next hill beyond the woods, and that they forced him to retire. I ordered my brigade forward through the woods in line of battle skirting the Mill Springs road. The march of the 2nd Minnesota was soon obstructed by the 10th Indiana, which was scattered through the woods waiting for ammunition. In front of them I saw the 4th Kentucky engaging the enemy, but evidently retiring. At this moment the enemy with shouts advanced on them about 100 yards and took position within the field on the hilltop near the second fence from the woods. At this time I received your order to advance as rapidly as possible to the hilltop. I ordered the 2nd Minnesota Regiment to move by the flank until it passed the 10th Indiana and 4th Kentucky and then deploy to the left of the road. I ordered the 9th Ohio to move through the first corn field to the right of the road and take position at the farther fence, selecting the best cover possible. The position of the 2nd Minnesota Regiment covered the ground formerly occupied by the 4th Kentucky and 10th Indiana, which brought their right flank within about ten feet of the enemy where he had advanced upon the 4th Kentucky. The 9th Ohio position checked an attempt on the part of the enemy to flank the position taken by the 2nd Minnesota and consequently brought the left wing almost against the enemy, where he was stationed behind straw stacks and piles of fence rails. Another regiment was stationed immediately in front of the 9th Ohio, well covered by a fence and some woods, a small field not more than sixty yards wide, intervening between the positions. The enemy also had possession of a small log house, stable and corn-crib, about fifty yards in front of the 9th Ohio.

Along the lines of each of the regiments, and from the enemy's front a hot and deadly fire opened. On the right wing of the 2nd Minnesota regiment the contest was at first almost hand-to-hand; the enemy and the 2nd Minnesota were poking their guns through the same fence. However, before the fight continued long in this way, that part of the enemy contending with the 2nd Minnesota regiment, retired in good order to some rail piles hastily thrown together, the point from which they had advanced upon the 4th Kentucky. This portion of the enemy obstinately maintaining their position and the balance remaining as before described, a desperate fire was continued for about thirty minutes, with seemingly doubtful results. The importance of possessing the log house, stable and corn-crib soon became apparent and companies A, B, C and D, of the 9th Ohio were ordered to flank the enemy upon the extreme left and obtain possession of the house. This done, still the enemy stood firm to his position and cover. During this time the artillery of the enemy constantly overshot my brigade. Seeing the superior number of the enemy and their bravery, I concluded the best mode of settling the contest was to order the 9th Ohio regiment to charge the enemy's position with the bayonet and turn his left flank. The order was given the regiment to empty their guns and fix bayonets; this done, it was ordered to charge. Every man sprang to it with alacrity and vociferous cheering, the enemy seemingly prepared to resist it, but before the regiment reached him the lines began to give way. But few of them stood, possibly ten or twelve.

This broke the enemy's flank and the whole line gave way in great confusion, and the whole turned into a perfect rout. As soon as I could form the regiments of my brigade I pursued the enemy to the hospital, where you joined the advance. I then moved my command forward under orders in line of battle to the foot of Moulden's Hill, passing on the way one abandoned cannon.

The next morning we marched into the deserted works of the enemy, and on the following day returned to our camp. At the time of the first advance of the 9th Ohio, I was shot through the right leg below the knee. Three other balls passed through my horse and another through my overcoat. After this I was compelled to go on foot till I got to the hospital of the enemy. About the time I was shot in the leg aid-de-camp Andrew S. Burt was shot in the side.

Too much praise cannot be awarded to the company officers, non-commissioned officers and the soldiers of the two regiments. Notwithstanding they had been called out before breakfast and had not tasted food all day, they conducted themselves throughout like veterans, obeying each command and executing every movement as though they were on parade. Although all the officers of the command evinced the greatest courage and deported themselves under fire in a proper soldierly manner, were I to fail to specify some of them, it would be great injustice. Lieut. Andrew S. Burt, aid-de-camp, of the 18th U. S. infantry; Hunter Brooke, private of the 2nd Minnesota regiment and volunteer aid-de-camp, Maj. Gustave Kammerling commanding the 9th Ohio; Capt. Charles Joseph, Co. A; Capt. Fredrick Shroder, Co. D; Geo. H. Harries, Adjutant, of the 9th Ohio regiment; Col. H. P. Van Cleve, James George, Lieut. Col. Alex. Wilkin, Major of 2nd Minnnesota, each displayed great valor and judgment in the discharge of their respective duties, so much so, in my judgment, as to place the country and every honest friend thereof under obligations to them.

In conclusion, permit me, sir, to congratulate you upon the victory achieved and allow me to express the hope that your future efforts will be crowned with the same success.

Attached you will find the number of the force of my brigade engaged, and also a list of the killed and wounded.

I am respectfully yours,

Rob't. L. McCook,

Col. 9th Ohio Regiment.

Commanding 3rd Brigade, 1st Division, Dept. of Ohio. Brig. Gen. Geo. H. Thomas, commanding 1st Division.

[No. 12.]

Report of Gen. Geo. H. Thomas, commanding division.
(*War of Rebellion, Official Records, Series 1, Vol. 7, page 79.*)

HEADQUARTERS 1ST DIVISION,
DEPARTMENT OF THE OHIO.
SOMERSET, KY., January 31st, 1862.

CAPTAIN:—I have the honor to report that in carrying out the instructions of the general commanding the department, contained in his communication of the 29th of December, I reached Logan's cross roads, about ten miles north of the entrenched camp of the enemy on the Cumberland river, on the 17th inst., with a portion of the 2nd and 3rd brigades, Kenny's battery of artillery, and a battalion of Wolford's cavalry.

* * * * * * * *

About 6:30 o'clock on the morning of the 19th the pickets from Wolford's cavalry encountered the enemy advancing on our camp, retired slowly and reported their advance to Col. M. D. Manson, commanding the 2nd brigade He immediately formed his regiment, the 10th Indiana, and took a position on the road to await the attack, ordering the 4th Kentucky (Col. S. S. Fry) to support him, and then informed me in person that the enemy were advancing in force, and what disposition he had made to resist him. I directed him to join the brigade immediately and hold the enemy in check until I could order up the other troops, which were ordered to form immediately and were marching towards the field in ten minutes afterwards. The battalion of Michigan engineers and Company "A," 38th Ohio (Capt. Greenwood), were ordered to remain as guards to the camp.

Upon my arrival on the field soon afterwards I found the 10th Indiana formed in front of their encampment, apparently awaiting orders, and ordered them forward to the support of the 4th Kentucky, which was the only entire regiment then engaged. I then rode forward myself to see the enemy's position, so that I could determine what disposition to make of my troops as they arrived. On reaching the position held by the 4th Kentucky, 10th Indiana and Wolford's cavalry, at a point where the roads fork leading to Somerset, I found the enemy advancing through a cornfield and evidently endeavoring to gain the left of the 4th Kentucky regiment, which was maintaining its position in a most determined manner. I directed one of my aides to ride back and order up a section of artillery and the Tennessee brigade to advance upon the enemy's right, and sent orders for Col. McCook to advance with his two regiments, 9th Ohio and 2nd Minnesota, to support the 4th Kentucky and 10th Indiana.

A section of Capt. Kenny's battery took position on the edge of the field to the left of the 4th Kentucky, and opened an efficient fire on a regiment of Alabamians which were advancing on the 4th Kentucky. Soon afterwards the 2nd Minnesota (Col. H. P. Van Cleve) arrived, the Colonel reporting to me for instructions. I directed him to take the position of the 4th Kentucky and 10th Indiana, which regiments were nearly out of ammunition. The 9th Ohio, under the immediate command of Maj. Kammerling, came into position on the right of the road at the same time.

Immediately after these regiments had gained their positions the enemy opened a most determined and galling fire, which was returned by our troops in the same spirit, and for nearly half an hour the contest was maintained on both sides in the most obstinate manner. At this time the 12th Kentucky (Col. W. A. Hoskins) and the Tennessee brigade reached the field, to the left of the Minnesota regiment, and opened fire on the right flank of the enemy, who then began to fall back. The 2nd Minnesota kept up a most galling fire in front and the 9th Ohio charged the enemy on the right with bayonets fixed, turned their flank and drove them from the field, the whole line giving away and retreating in the utmost disorder and confusion. As soon as the regiments could be formed and refill their cartridge boxes, I ordered the whole force to advance. A few miles in the rear of the battlefield a small force of cavalry was drawn up near the road, but a few shots from our artillery (a section of Standart's battery) dispersed them, and none of the enemy were seen again until we arrived in front of their intrenchments. As we approached their intrenchments the division was deployed in line of battle and steadily advanced to the summit of the hill at Moulden's. From this point I directed their intrenchments to be cannonaded, which was done until dark by Standart's and Wetmore's batteries. Kenny's battery was placed in position on the extreme left, near Russell's house, from which point he was directed to fire on their ferry, to deter them from attempting to cross. On the following morning Capt. Wetmore's battery was ordered to Russell's house, and assisted with his Parrot guns in firing upon the ferry. Col. Manson's brigade took position on the left, near Kenny's battery, and every preparation was made to assault their intrenchments on the following morning. The 14th Ohio (Colonel Steedman) and the 10th Kentucky (Colonel Harlan) having joined from detached service soon after the repulse of the enemy, continued with their brigade in the pursuit, although they could not get up in time to join in the fight. These two regiments were placed in front in my advance on the intrenchment the next morning, and entered first. General Schoepf also joined me the evening of the 19th with the 17th, 31st and 38th Ohio. His entire brigade entered with the other troops.

On reaching the intrenchments we found that the enemy had abandoned everything and retired during the night. Twelve pieces of artillery with their caissons packed with ammunition, one battery wagon and two forges, a large amount of ammunition, a large number of small arms, mostly the old flint-lock muskets; 150 or 160 wagons, and upwards of 1,000 horses and mules; a large amount of commissary stores, intrenching tools and camp and garrison equipage, fell into our hands. A correct list of all the captured property will be forwarded as soon as it can be made up and the property secured.

The steam and ferry boats having been burned by the enemy in their retreat, it was found impossible to cross the river and pursue them; besides, their command was completely demoralized, and retreated in great haste and in all directions, making the capture in any numbers quite doubtful if pursued. There is no doubt but what the moral effect produced by their complete dispersion will have a more decided effect in re-establishing Union sentiments than though they had been captured. It affords me much pleasure to be able to testify to the uniform steadiness and good conduct of both officers and men during the battle, and I respectfully refer to the accompanying reports of the different commanders for the names of those officers and men whose good conduct was particularly noticed by them.

I regret to have to report that Col. R. L. McCook, commanding the 3rd brigade, and his aide, A. S. Burt, 18th U. S. Infantry, were both severely wounded in the first advance of the 9th Ohio regiment, but continued on duty until the brigade returned to camp at Logan's cross roads.

Col. S. S. Fry, 4th Kentucky, was slightly wounded, whilst his regiment was gallantly resisting the advance of the enemy, during which time Gen Zollicoffer fell from a shot from his (Col. Fry's) pistol, which no doubt contributed materially to the discomfiture of the enemy.

* * * * * * *

The enemy's loss as far as known is as follows: Brigadier General Zollicoffer, Lieut. Bailie Peyton and 190 officers, non-commissioned officers and privates killed; Lieut. Col. M. B. Carter, Twentieth Tennessee; Lieut. J. W. Allen, Fifteenth Mississippi; Lieut. Allen Morse, Sixteenth Alabama, and five officers of the medical staff and 81 non-commissioned officers and privates taken prisoners; Lieut. J. E. Patterson, Twentieth Tennessee, and A. J. Knapp, Fifteenth Mississippi, and 66 non-commissioned officers and privates, wounded, making 192 killed, 89 prisoners not wounded and 68 wounded; total of killed, wounded and prisoners, 349.

(NOTE—Crittenden reports 408 wounded and missing, which with the 192 dead, buried by Thomas, makes the enemy's loss 600.)

Our loss as follows:

Troops.	Killed.		Wounded.	
	Officers.	Men.	Officers.	Men.
10th Indiana		10	3	72
1st Kentucky, Cavalry	1	2		19
4th Kentucky		8	4	48
2nd Minnesota		12	2	31
9th Ohio		6	4	24
Total	1	38	13	194

A complete list of the names of our killed and wounded and of the prisoners is herewith attached.

I am, sir, very respectfully, your obedient servant,

GEO. H. THOMAS,

Brigadier General U. S. Volunteers, Commanding.

Capt. J. B. FRY, A. A. G.,

Chief of Staff, Headquarters, Dept. of Ohio, Louisville, Ky.

(No. 13.)

INSPECTION REPORT.

(Official Files, Adjutant General's Office, State of Minnesota.)

HEADQUARTERS DEPARTMENT OF THE CUMBERLAND,
  MURFREESBORO, TENN., February 7th, 1863.

SIR:—The General commanding desires me to state that he is extremely gratified to learn, that your regiment is among the number, who may be held up as an example worthy of imitation. Men who submit to discipline cheerfully, and take soldier's pride in their "personnel," he feels confident can be relied upon in an emergency.

The General desires you to read this letter on parade.

I am, sir, very respectfully your obedient servant,
  (Signed)   JAMES CURTIS,
Captain 15th U. S. Infantry and A. A. Inspecting General.
To COL. GEORGE,
  Commanding 2nd Minnesota Volunteers.

[No. 14.]

COMPLIMENTARY ORDERS.

(Published in St. Paul Pioneer, February 28th 1863.)

HEADQUARTERS 3RD BRIGADE,
  NEAR NOLINSVILLE, TENN., February, 1863.

The Colonel commanding the brigade, takes pleasure in commending the conduct and sturdy valor of Lovilo N. Holmes and fourteen non-commissioned officers and privates of Company H, 2nd Regiment Minnesota Volunteers, for the heroic defense made by them near Nolinsville on the 15th inst., against the attack of two companies of rebel cavalry numbering one hundred and twenty-five men, and repulsing them with loss.

This little affair is one of the most creditable of the campaign and deserves to be remembered and cited as worthy the emulation of all.

The Colonel desires that the names of these worthy men and brave soldiers may be preserved.

First Sergeant Lovilo N. Holmes.
Corporals Samuel Wright and William A. Clark,

Privates Nelson Crandall, James Flannigan, Samuel Leslie, Louis Londrash, Charles Liscomb, Joseph Burger, Byron E. Pay, Charles Krause, John Vale, Samuel Loudon, Milton Hanna and Homer Barnard, have his thanks.

By order of F. VAN DERVEER,
Colonel commanding 3rd Brigade.

JOHN R. BEATTY,
A. A. Adjutant General.

[No. 15.]

GENERAL STEEDMAN'S REPORT.

(Refers to No. 14.)

(*War of Rebellion, Official Records, Vol. 22, Part 1, page 49, Series 1.*)

REPORT OF BRIG. GEN'L JAMES B. STEEDMAN.

CONCORD CHURCH, February 15th, 1863.

COLONEL:—A forage train of ten wagons from my command, with escort of two companies of infantry; and while four of the wagons guarded by 13 privates under the command of a Sergeant, were being loaded one and a half miles from Nolinsville, were attacked by one hundred and fifty rebel cavalry. The Sergeant immediately formed his men, took shelter in a cabin near the wagons and repulsed them, wounding five, three of whom I have prisoners, killing four horses, capturing three horses, seven saddles and three guns. Two of our men were slightly wounded.

*   *   *   *   *   *   *   *

Very respectfully,
JAMES B. STEEDMAN,
Brigadier General Third Division.

COLONEL. C. GODDARD,
Assistant Adjutant General and Chief of Staff.

[No. 16.]

BATTLES OF CHICAMAUGA.

Report of Col. James George, commanding regiment.

(*Official Files, Adjutant General's Office, State of Minnesota.*)

HEADQUARTERS 2ND REGIMENT,
MINNESOTA VOLUNTEERS.
CHATTANOOGA, TENN. Sept. 25, 1863.

GENERAL:—I have the honor to transmit the following report of the part taken by the 2nd regiment of Minnesota volunteers in the battles of the 19th and 20th inst. near Crawfish Spring, Georgia:

The regiment was placed in position at ten o'clock A. M. on the 19th on the extreme left of the brigade and next battery "I" 4th U. S. artillery, facing the south. A few minutes later the enemy approached in front in line to about 300 yards and opened a heavy fire of musketry, which was returned with such effect as to repulse the attack; in about ten minutes another attack was soon after made and met with a like repulse, the enemy falling back in disorder, entirely out of sight.

About half-past ten o'clock sharp firing of musketry was suddenly opened at some distance in our left and front which soon began to approach us. The cartridge boxes had been replenished, and the regiment was laid down in line to await its time; the men having been admonished to withhold their fire until the enemy should be within close range.

There soon appeared approaching in disorder from the left front a line of our troops in full retreat and closely pursued by the enemy who was cheering and firing furiously in their rear. It proved to be the regular brigade, the men of which passed over our line and were afterwards partially rallied in our rear and on our left.

As soon as these troops had passed us, the further advance of the enemy was checked by a volley from our line. A sharp contest with musketry followed which resulted in a few minutes in the complete repulse of the late exultant enemy, who fled from our front in confusion.

About eleven o'clock a large force was discovered advancing on us from the east and simultaneously from the north. Our front was immediately changed to the left to meet this attack, and after a few minutes fighting the enemy seeming to be moved around to the northward; our front was again changed to the left, under a hot fire, so that the regiment faced the northeast, and again finally to face the north as the enemy massed his troops for an assault from that direction. The enemy charged desperately and were finally completely repulsed and routed after a brief but bloody contest.

The fighting ended with us at about 11:30 A. M. Our loss was eight killed and forty-one wounded, including two commissioned officers. None missing. The regiment commenced the battle with 384 officers and enlisted men.

On the 20th the regiment took place in the brigade with 295 officers and men, forty men having been detached for picket duty the previous evening and not relieved when the regiment marched.

At ten A. M. the regiment, on the right of the brigade was advanced into an open field to the support of a battery which was in action immediately on our right, the line facing the east. Scarcely had the line been halted in its assigned place when a furious fire of musketry and artillery was opened on it from the edge of woods bordering the field on the north and 300 or 400 yards distant. The brigade front was instantly changed to the left, the movement being made in good order, though under fire, and our line at once opened on the enemy. After a few minutes firing a charge was ordered, and we advanced on the double-quick across the field and into the woods, driving the enemy back upon their supports. Here the engagement was continued for fifteen or twenty minutes, when the enemy moved off by their right flank, clearing our front and getting out of our range, even when firing left oblique. The regiment was then withdrawn, and the brigade reformed facing north.

Presently an artillery fire was opened on us from the east, and our front was changed to face it. After remaining here in position for about half an hour, we were moved off a distance of a mile or more to a hill on the right of our general line of battle, where at 2:30 P. M. we again became hotly engaged with musketry. The enemy charged repeatedly and desperately on our position here, but were repulsed by the cool and deadly fire of our rifles; the firing here continued without intermission until 4:45 P. M., when the enemy temporarily withdrew from the contest. Two other attacks were afterwards made on us here, but both were repulsed and darkness ended the fight at about 6:30 P. M.

Our loss on this day was twenty-seven killed and seventy-two wounded, being more than one-third of our entire number. None missing. Some eight or ten men of other commands who joined us temporarily were killed while bravely fighting in our ranks. I regret that I cannot give their names and regiments.

The conduct of the officers and men of my regiment was on both days uniformly gallant and soldier-like beyond praise. If any one of them failed in doing his whole duty I do not know it.

Assistant Surgeon Otis Ayer, and Hospital Steward A. Buckingham, were captured from field hospital Sept. 20, and are prisoners in the hands of the enemy. A good portion of our wounded men were left lying on the field and are now prisoners in hands of the enemy.

I am General, very respectfully,
Your most obedient servant,
JAS. GEORGE,
Commanding 2nd Minn. Vols.

[No. 17.]

BATTLES OF CHICAMAUGA.

List of the killed and wounded in the Second Regiment, Minnesota Vols., during the late battles near Chattanooga, Tenn., Sept. 19th and 20th, 1863.

(*Official Files, Adjutant General's Office, State of Minnesota.*)

Name.	Rank and Co.		Nature of Wound.
John B. Davis	Major		Flesh wound, temple.
Peter G. Wheeler	Sergt. Maj.		Flesh wound, chin.
Abram Kalder	Sergt.	A	Slight, in arm.
Thos. Fitch	Corpl.	A	Severely, in nose and arm.
M. D. E. Runals	Private	A	Severely, in left lung.
Ozias M. Work	"	A	Severely, in body and leg.
Eben E. Corliss	"	A	Slight, in head.
Chas. A. Edwards	"	A	Slight, in hand.
Manley S. Harris	"	A	Slight, in hand.
D. M. Morse	"	A	Severely, in face and arm.
Chas. A. Rouse	"	A	Severely, in head.
Fred. H. Russell	"	A	Severely, in arm.
Robt. Smalley	"	A	Severely, in body.
Abram Harkins	Captain	B	Comp. fracture, right arm
M. V. Dietre	Corpl.	B	Severely, in leg.
A. V. Doty	Private	B	Fracture, left leg.
John L. Kenney	"	B	Severely, in leg.
Granville Farrier	"	B	Severely, in leg.
Wm. Swan	"	B	Severely, in arm.
Manning Bailey	"	B	Slight, in hand.
E. V. Comstock	"	B	Slight, in hand.
F. Kelsey	"	B	Slight, in shoulder.
Chas. Lane	"	B	Slight, in shoulder.
C. J. Lange	"	B	Slight, in head.
J. C. Kitchell	"	B	Slight, in arm.
David Bush	"	B	Slight, in shoulder.
H. G. Smith	"	B	Slight, in head.

Name.	Rank and Co.		Nature of Wound.
M. Thoeny	2nd Lieut.	C	Slight, in wrist.
Wm. Mills	1st Lieut.	C	Slight, in arm.
M. L. Devereaux	Sergt.	C	Slight, in shoulder.
J. J. Casseday	Corpl.	C	Slight, in hip.
A. Hochstetter	"	C	Slight, in head.
P. Grunenwald	"	C	Slight, in left side,
C. Matti	"	C	Severely, in leg.
M. Rowhan	"	C	Slight, in foot.
T. D. Orcutt	"	C	Slight, in leg.
G. H. Ames	Private	C	Slight, in leg.
J. B. Gere	"	C	Mortal, in both knees.
John Fern	"	C	Slight, in arm.
C. Alden	"	C	Slight, in leg.
D. C. Morgan	"	C	Slight, in leg.
A. R. Hall	Sergt.	D	Severely, in breast.
S. B. Holship	"	D	Slight, in head.
E. B. Nettleton	Corpl.	D	Slight, in arm.
G. M. Gilchrist	Private	D	Severely, in body.
W. H. Wiley	"	D	Severely, in head.
G. W. Fowler	"	D	Severely, in hand.
John Spring	"	D	Severely, in hip.
Felix Carriveau	"	D	Severely, in hands.
Henry Vessey	"	D	Severely, in leg.
Chas. Clewett	"	D	Severely, in arm.
Ben Sylvester	1st Sergt.	E	Severely, in left arm.
A. A. Stone	Sergt.	E	Severely, in leg and hip.
Solon Cheadle	Corpl.	E	Slightly, in foot.
Nicholas Sons	"	E	Slightly, in leg.
Eli Huggins	"	E	Severely, in wrist.
I. W. French	Private	E	Severely, in shoulder.
James Flora	"	E	Severely, in side.
James Spencer	"	E	Severely, in both legs.
Lewis Swenson	"	E	Slightly, in shoulder.
James Smith	"	E	Slightly, in arm.
Joseph Smith	"	E	Slightly, in side.
Peter M. Freteuff	"	E	Severely, in hand.
Samuel Bowler	"	E	Severely, in leg.
W. L. Jones	"	E	Severely, in shoulder.
Edwin Knudson	"	E	Slightly, in head.
Benj. Warrant	"	E	Severely, in hips.
G. W. Wallace	1st Sergt.	F	Severely, in right shoulder
Paul Caviezell	Sergt.	F	Slightly, in thigh.
Henry Oaks	Private	F	Severely, in head.
Thos. A. Tiernan	"	F	Severely, in foot.

Name.	Rank and Co.		Nature of Wound.
Jas. M. Thornton	Private	F	Severely, in foot.
Joseph Bird	"	F	Slightly, in thigh.
Michael McCarthy	"	F	Slightly, in leg.
H. V. Rumohr	1st Sergt.	G	Severely, in nose.
J. A. Smith	Corpl.	G	Severely, in arm.
Henry Bush	"	G	Slightly, in
Peter Douthiel	Private	G	Severely, in shoulder.
Peter Freyman	"	G	Severely, in head.
Chas. Janke	"	G	Severely, in hands and leg.
Geo. Reed	"	G	Slightly, in thigh.
Batens Weber	"	G	Severely, in side.
Thos. G. Quayle	2nd Lieut.	H	Slightly, in left hip.
Josiah Keene	Sergt.	H	Severely, in left arm.
Milton Hanna	Corp.	H	Severely, in leg.
John S. Hilliard	"	H	Severely, in leg.
A. B. Rose	"	H	Mortally, in hip.
Saml. Loudon	Private	H	Slightly, in leg.
S. A. Mitchell	"	H	Severely, in leg.
Chas. Krause	"	H	Mortally, in body.
Byron E. Pay	"	H	Severely, in shoulder.
Cyrus W. Smith	"	H	Severely, in arm and foot.
Lewis Londrosh	"	H	Slightly, in hand.
E. T. Cressey	"	H	Slightly, in shoulder.
Albert Gesel	"	H	Slightly, in foot.
Albert Parker	Corpl.	I	Severely, in thigh.
Adam Wickert	"	I	Slightly, in side.
H. T. Whipple	Private	I	Severely, in foot.
W. S. Wells	"	I	Severely, in thigh.
C. C. Handy	"	I	Slightly, in finger.
Isaac Layman	"	I	Severely, in arm.
D. S. Coverdale	2nd Lieut.	K	Slightly, in left hip.
John R. Barber	Corpl.	K	Slightly, in finger.
Robt. McClellan	Private	K	Mortally, in body.
Edwin Baird	"	K	Severely, in arm.
V. R. Barton	"	K	Severely, in hand and leg.
Lyman S. Martin	"	K	Severely, in arm.
John McAlpin	"	K	Severely, in body and leg.
Henry Roberts	"	K	Severely, in side.
John Shouts	"	K	Severely, in side.
Wm. Hamilton	"	K	Severely, in wrist.
John C. Smith	"	K	Severely, in shoulder.
Samuel Fleming	"	K	Slightly, in knee.
Chas. Fewster	1st Sergt.	A	Killed.
Norman E. Case	Corpl.	A	"

Name.	Rank and Co.		Nature of Wound.
C. S. Cutting	Corpl.	B	Killed.
S. D. Calvert	Private	B	"
A. H. Palmer	"	B	"
S. Taylor	"	B	"
F. I. Crabb	"	B	"
J. McAuliff	Sergt.	C	"
Jacob Martig	Private	C	"
C. Schilt	"	C	"
S. B. Neros	"	C	"
Wm. Dudley	Sergt.	D	"
John Sherburne	Corp.	D	"
Alfonso Bogan	Private	D	"
Geo. H. Fry	1st Sergt.	F	"
D. B. Griffin	Corpl.	F	"
Cornelius Holland	Private	F	"
Herman Raduentz	"	G	"
Charles Schuele	"	G	"
Jacob Seibert	"	G	"
Francis T. Satorius	"	G	"
John M. Foster	Sergt.	H	"
Nicholas Weiss	Corpl.	H	" (wounded only.)
John B. Hopewell	Private	H	"
Alfred W. Bigelow	"	H	"
Wm. H. Weagunt	"	H	"
Arnold Cochrane	Corpl.	I	"
Wardwell Mathers	Private	I	"
Wm. McCurdy	"	I	"
Joseph Shonmaker	"	I	"
Freeman Schneider	"	I	"
I. B. Pomeroy	Sergt.	K	"
Alex. Metzger	Corpl.	K	"
John A. Cutting	Private	K	"
Jas. A. Bigelow	"	K	"

```
Total commissioned officers wounded........   6
Total enlisted men wounded..................  107
Total enlisted men killed...................   35
                                              ---
Total loss..................................  148
Assistant Surgeon Otis Ayer and Hospital
  Steward, F. Buckingham captured at field
  hospital .................................    2
```

The above is as complete a list of the casualities of the 2nd Minnesota regiment as can be obtained at the present time;

many of those wounded in the second day's fight were left in the enemy's hands. The regiment behaved most gallantly, not a man left the ranks but that was known to be either killed or wounded. The wounded at this place are doing well, and are as comfortable as could be expected.

Lt. Albert Woodbury, 2nd Minnesota Battery, is here, severely wounded in the left arm above the elbow joint.

I remain, yours truly,
M. C. TOLMAN,
Surgeon 2nd Minnesota Volunteers,
Medical Director 3rd Division, 14th A. C., D. C.

These men were detailed to care for our wounded men and were captured in performing that duty:

George A. Baker, private, Co. B.
Jediah Furman,   "   " B.
Hiram A. Stewart,   "   " B.
Ashley W. Wood,   "   " B.
John Stuckey,   "   " C.
Charles Sweeney,   "   " C.
Peter Walrick,   "   " C.
Washington Maguire,   "   " D.
Henry Oaks,   "   " F.
Uriah S. Karmany,   "   " H.
John S. Bertrand,   "   " I.
William B. Haskin,   "   " K.
—— 12 captured.

Total loss 162, 42 2-10 per cent of 384 men engaged.

(No. 18.)

BATTLE OF CHICAMAUGA.

Supplementary report by COL. JAMES GEORGE.

(*Adjutant General's Report for 1863, State of Minnesota*).

HEADQUARTERS SECOND MINNESOTA
REGIMENT VOLUNTEERS,
CHATTANOOGA, Tennessee, September 30, 1863.

GENERAL:—For the purpose of placing on record the names of those officers and men, who for gallant and meritorious conduct on the battlefield of the Chicamauga are entitled to special mention, I respectfully submit the following list as supplementary to the general report of the operations of my regiment, a copy of which has already been transmitted to your office.

I am under special obligations to my staff and field officers. More praiseworthy exhibitions of coolness and courage under fire were never made upon any field of battle. They each deserve much of their country, not only for their gallant conduct in these battles, but for their uniform industry and ability in the faithful discharge of every duty. Such officers are a credit to the State and to the service.

Lieut. Col. J. W. Bishop had his horse shot under him in the second day's battle, but kept his place on foot, it being impossible at the time to get a re-mount.

Major John B. Davis also had his horse shot under him, and was soon after wounded in the forehead with a fragment of shell, but kept his post during the battle, which lasted several hours afterwards.

Adjutant James W. Wood had his horse shot under him, but continued in the active discharge of his duty on foot.

Assistant Surgeon William Brown was engaged in dressing the wounded on the field, and frequently under fire both days.

Assistant Surgeon Otis Ayer remained at his post attending to our wounded, and while thus in the discharge of his duty became a prisoner. He was afterwards exchanged and has re-joined his regiment.

Of the company officers, there were present with their respective companies, and each in the energetic, faithful and fearless discharge of his duty, the following:

Capt. Abraham Harkins, Co. B, severely wounded 2nd day.
Capt. John Moulton, " D.
Capt. J. C. Donahower, " E.
Capt. D. B. Loomis, " F.
Capt. C. F. Meyer, " G.
Capt. C. S. Uline, " I.
Capt. W. W. Woodbury, " K.
1st Lieut. Levi Ober, " A, commanding his company.
1st Lieut. W. W. Wilson, " B.
1st Lieut. H. K. Couse, " C, commanding his company.
1st Lieut. S. G. Trimble, " D.
1st Lieut. J. S. Livingston," F.
1st Lieut. H. V. Rumohr, " G, wounded in face 2nd day.
1st Lieut. L. N. Holmes, " H, commanding his company.
1st Lieut. Tenbroeck Stout," I.
2nd Lieut. E. L. Kenny, " A.
2nd Lieut. M. Thoeny, " C, wounded in hand 1st day.
2nd Lieut. H. Lobdell, " D.
2nd Lieut. T. G. Scott, " E.
2nd Lieut. T. G. Quale, " H, wounded in hip 2nd day.
2nd Lieut. D. S. Coverdale," K, wounded in thigh 1st day.

Sergt. Maj. P. C. Wheeler was slightly wounded in the chin the first day.

Orderly M. D. E. Runals and bugler Albert Gsell are entitled to special mention for their gallant and prompt discharge of their duties, under fire. Both were severely wounded.

The following named men are also reported to me by their company commanders as having specially distinguished themselves in the line of duty, on the battlefield, while without exception, all present are credited with gallant and soldier-like conduct:

Sergeant Alonzo Worden, Corporal A. McCorkle, and Private James W. Stewart, of Company A.

Sergeants John McAuliff and Robert S. Hutchinson and Private James B. Gere, of Company C.

Sergeants Albert R. Hall and Rollin A. Lampher and Private Gideon M. Gilchrist, of Company D.

Sergeant Benjamin Sylvester, Corporal O. P. Renne and Private Michael Horrigan, of Company E.

Corporal John A. Smith and Privates Janke and Weber, of Company G.

Private William S. Wells, of Company I.

Sergeants A. H. Reed and John D. Burr and Private William B. C. Evans, of Company K.

Very respectfully yours, etc.,

OSCAR MALMROS,   J. GEORGE,
   Adjutant General.   Colonel Commanding
     State of Minnesota.   2nd Minnesota Volunteers.

(No. 19.)

BATTLE OF CHICAMAUGA.

Report of COL. F. VAN DERVEER, commanding Brigade:

(Official Files, Adjutant General's Office, State of Minnesota.)

HEADQUARTERS 3RD BRIGADE,
3RD DIVISION, 14TH A. C.,
CHATTANOOGA, Tenn., Sept. 25th, 1863.

Capt. Louis J. Lambert, A. A. G.:

CAPTAIN:—I have the honor to report the part taken by the 3rd Brigade in the actions of the 19th and 20th inst., near the Chicamauga. My command consisted of the 2nd Minnesota, Col. George; the 9th Ohio, Col. Kammerling; the 35th Ohio, Lt. Col. Boynton; the 87th Indiana, Col.

Gleason; and Battery "I," 4th Artillery, 1st Lt. F. G. Smith. Our effective strength on the morning of the 19th inst., was 1,788 officers and men.

After a fatiguing march during the night of the 18th, and without any sleep or rest, whilst halting near Kelly's house on the Rossville and Lafayette road, I received an order from Brig. Gen. Brannan, commanding the 3rd Division, to move with haste along the road to Reed's bridge over the Chicamauga, take possession of a ford near that point and hold it. I immediately moved southward to McDaniel's house, and thence at right angles eastwardly toward the bridge. A short distance from McDaniel's I formed the brigade into two lines, sent skirmishers to the front and advanced cautiously, though without losing time, one and one-half miles. In the meantime brisk firing was progressing on my right, understood to be maintained by the 1st and 2nd Brigades of this Division.

Being without a guide and entirely unacquainted with the country, I am unable to state how near I went to Reed's bridge, but perceiving from the firing on my right that I was passing the enemy's flank, I wheeled my line in that direction and began feeling his position with my skirmishers. About this time I received an order, stating that the 2nd brigade was gradually giving back, and that it was necessary I should at once make an attack. This we did with a will; the first line, composed of the 35th Ohio on the right, and the 2nd Minnesota on the left, moving down a gentle slope, leaving the 87th Indiana in reserve on the crest of the hill.

At this time the 9th Ohio, which had charge of the ammunition train of the division, had not arrived. Smith's battery, composed of four twelve-pound Napoleons, were placed in position in the centre and on the right of the line. The enemy having discovered our position opened a furious fire of artillery and musketry, which was replied to promptly and apparently with considerable effect, for in half an hour the enemy slackened his fire and his advance line was compelled to fall back. I took advantage of this movement to bring forward the 87th Indiana, and by a passage of lines to the front carried them to the relief of the 35th Ohio, which had already suffered severely in the engagement. This movement was executed with as much coolness and accuracy as if on drill. Scarcely was the 87th Indiana in line before fresh forces of the enemy were brought up, in time to receive from us a terrible volley which made his ranks stagger and held him some time at bay.

The 9th Ohio, which I had previously sent for, arrived at this moment. I placed it on the right of my line. Still further to the right a section of Church's battery and the 17th Ohio, which had been ordered to report to me, were in position as the enemy slackened their fire. Col. Kammerling, chafing like a wounded tiger that he had been behind at the opening, ordered his men to charge; away they went, closely followed by the 87th Indiana and 17th Ohio, the enemy falling back precipitately. The 9th in this charge recaptured the guns in Guenther's battery, 5th artillery, and held them.

In the meantime the enemy, massing his forces suddenly, appeared upon my left and rear; he came forward several lines deep at a double-quick, and opened a brisk fire, but not before I had changed my front to resist him. My new line consisted of the 2nd Minnesota on the right, next one section of Smith's battery, commanded by Lieut. Rodney, then the 87th Indiana, flanked by Church's and the other sections of Smith's battery, and on the extreme left the 35th Ohio. The two extremities of the line formed an obtuse angle, the vertex on the left of the 87th Indiana, and the opening toward the enemy. The 2nd Minnesota and 87th Indiana lay on the ground and were apparently unobserved by the enemy, who moved upon the left of my lines, delivering and receiving a direct fire. Church opened with all his guns, and Smith with one section. He advanced rapidly, my left giving way slowly until his flank was brought opposite my right wing, when a murderous and enfilading fire was poured into his ranks by the infantry and by Rodney's section shotted with canister. Notwithstanding this, he moved steadily up his second and third lines.

Having observed his great force as well as the persistency of his attack, I had sent messenger after messenger to bring up the 9th Ohio, which had not yet returned from its charge made from my original site. At last, however, and when it seemed impossible for my brave men to longer withstand the impetuous advance of the enemy, the 9th came gallantly up in time to take part in the final struggle, which resulted in his sudden withdrawal. In this last attack his loss must have been very severe. In addition to the heavy fire of the infantry, our guns were pouring double charges of canister in front and on his flanks, at one time delivered at a distance of not exceeding forty (40) yards.

During the latter part of the contest reinforcements had arrived, and were by Gen. Brannan, then present, formed in line for the purpose of supporting my brigade, but were not actively engaged at this time. Our dead and wounded were gathered up and a new line, under the supervision of Gen. Brannan, was formed. The enemy, however, made no further demonstration, and quietly withdrew. A small number of prisoners were taken, who reported that the force opposed to us was two divisions of Longstreet's corps, one commanded by Gen. Hood. They fought with great obstinacy and determination, only retreating when fairly swept away by our overwhelming fire. After the second withdrawal by the enemy our empty cartridge boxes were replenished by wagons sent into the field by the General commanding the division.

After resting my command for an hour or more, I was ordered to report to Maj. Gen. Reynolds. Immediately moving towards his position, we arrived near Kelly's house just before sundown, and there, by direction of Gen. Brannan, went into bivouac.

At 8 o'clock the next morning, Sunday, the 20th Sept., 1863, my brigade was posted as a reserve in the rear of the 1st and 2nd brigades of the division, formed in two lines of columns closed in mass, where we remained for about an hour, slowly moving over towards the left for the purpose of occupying the space between the 3rd and Reynold's division. There I received an order to move quickly over to the left and support Gen. Baird who, it was said, was being hard pressed by the enemy. I wheeled my battalions to the left, deployed both lines and moved through the woods parallel to the Chattanooga road, gradually swinging round my left until, when in rear of Reynold's position, I struck the road perpendicularly at a point just north of Kelly's house, near and back of his lines.

On approaching the road, riding in advance of the brigade, my attention was called to a large force of the enemy moving southward in four lines, just then emerging from the woods at a run, evidently intending to attack Reynolds and Baird, who were both hotly engaged, in the rear, and apparently unseen by those officers. I immediately wheeled my lines to the left, facing the approaching force, and ordered them to lie down. This movement was not executed until we received a galling fire, delivered from a distance of two hundred (200) yards. At the same time a rebel battery placed in the road about five (5) or six (6) hundred yards in our front, opened upon us with two (2) guns. My command continued to lie down until the enemy approached within seventy-five (75) feet, and the front line, composed of the 2nd Minnesota and 87th Indiana, delivered a murderous fire almost in their faces, and the 35th and 9th Ohio, passing lines quickly to the front, the whole brigade charged and drove the enemy at a full run, over the open ground, for over a quarter of a mile, and several hundred yards into the woods; my men keeping in good order and delivering their fire as they advanced. The rebels fled hastily to cover, leaving the ground strewn with their dead and wounded.

We took position in the woods, and maintained a determined combat for more than an hour. At this time I greatly needed my battery, which had been taken from the brigade early in the day by command of Maj. Gen. Negley. Finding a force moving on our right to support us, and the enemy being almost silenced, I ordered return to the open grounds south of the woods; this movement was executed by passing lines to the rear, each line firing as it retired. I learned from prisoners that the force we fought and put to flight this day was the division of the rebel Gen. Breckenridge. That we punished them severely was proved by their many dead and wounded, among the former of which were several field officers, and among the latter one general officer of high rank.

I thence moved to a position on the road near Gen. Reynold's centre, and there remained resting my men and caring for my wounded for an hour or more. Although I had not reported to either Generals Reynolds or Baird, as ordered in the morning, I believe I rendered them very substantial assistance, and at a time when it was greatly needed.

About two o'clock, hearing heavy firing to the right of the line, and learning that the high ground in that direction was being held by Gen. Brannan with a part of our division, I moved cautiously through the woods, and at 2:30 P. M. reported my brigade to him for duty. We were immediately placed in the front, relieving his troops, then almost exhausted. The position was well selected and capable of being defended against a heavy force, the line being a crest of a hill, for the possession of which the enemy made most desperate and renewed attempts. From this time until dark we were hotly engaged. The ammunition failing and no supply on hand except a small quantity furnished by Maj. Gen. Gordon Granger, our men gathered their cartridges from the boxes of the dead, wounded and prisoners, and finally fixed bayonets, determined to hold the position. Here again the 9th Ohio made a gallant charge down the hill into the midst of the enemy, scattering them like chaff, and then returning to their position on the hill. For an hour and one-half before dark the attack was one of unexampled fury, line after line of fresh troops being hurled against our position with a heroism and persistency which almost dignified their cause. At length night ended the struggle and the enemy having suffered a terrible loss, retired from our immediate front.

During the latter part of the day the position directly on our right had been held by Brig. Gen. Steedman, but which, early in the evening had been withdrawn without our knowledge, thus leaving our flank exposed. From the silence at that point, Brig. Gen. Brannan suspected that all might not be right, and ordered me to place the 35th Ohio across that flank to prevent a surprise. This had scarcely been done before a rebel force appeared in the gloom directly in their front. A mounted officer rode to within a few paces of the 35th and asked "What regiment is that?" To this some one replied "The 35th Ohio." The officer turned suddenly and attempted to run away, but our regiment delivered a volley that brought horse and rider to the ground, and put to flight the force. Prisoners said this officer was the rebel Gen. Gregg.

At seven (7) o'clock P. M. an order came from Maj. Gen. Thomas that the forces under Gen. Brannan should move quietly to Rossville. This was carried into execution under the direction of Capt. Cilley, of my staff, in excellent order.

During the whole of the two days' fighting my brigade kept well together, at all times obeying orders promptly and moving with regularity and precision as if on drill. They were subjected to a very severe test on the 19th, when being actively engaged with the enemy, another brigade (not of our division) ran panic-stricken through and over us, some of the officers of which shouted to our men to retreat, or they would certainly be overwhelmed, but not a man left the ranks and the approaching enemy found before him a wall of steel. Private Savage, of Smith's battery struck one of the retreating officers with his sponge and damned him for running against his gun.

Our loss in the engagement of both days amounts to 13 officers and 132 men killed, and 25 officers and 581 men wounded and 51 missing. The total loss being 802 men and officers. Doubtless many of those enumerated among the missing will be found either wounded or killed. There was no straggling and I have no doubt those not wounded or killed will be found prisoners in the hands of the enemy. *It is a noticeable fact that the 2nd Minnesota had not a single man among the missing or a straggler, during the two days' engagement.*

I cannot speak too highly of the conduct of my officers and men; without exception they performed all that was required, much more than could have been expected.

Where all did so well, it seems almost unjust to make distinctions; more gallantry and indomitable courage was never displayed upon the field of battle.

The attention of the General commanding the division is particularly called to the conduct of Col. James George, commanding 2nd Minn. vols.; Col. Gustavus Kammerling, commanding 9th Ohio vols.; Col. N. Gleason, 87th Indiana vols.; Lt. Col. H. V. N. Boynton, commanding 35th Ohio vols.; and 1st Lieut. F. G. Smith, commanding battery "I," 4th U. S. artillery. These officers performed every duty required of them with coolness and great promptness, and by their energy and gallantry contributed much to the favorable result which attended every collision with the enemy.

Such officers are a credit to the service and our country. Smith's battery rendered great help in the action of the 19th inst., and was ably and gallantly served, Lieut. Rodney being conspicuous in the management of his section.

Capt. Church of the 1st brigade, with one section of his battery, fought well and is entitled to credit he rendered me on the 19th.

I cannot refrain from alluding to the reckless courage and dash of Adjt. Harris, of the 9th Ohio vols.

My staff upon the field consisted of Capt. J. R. Beatty, 2nd Minnesota vols.; A. A. A. G., Captains P. H. Parshall, 35th Ohio, and B. B. Thoenssen, 9th Ohio; acting aids, Capt. C. A. Cilley, 2nd Minn. vols., Brig. Topographical Engineer, and 1st Lt. A. E. Alden, 2nd Minn. vols., Brig. Inspector. For efficiency, personal bravery and energy, their conduct deserves more than praise. They exposed themselves at all times watching the movements of the enemy, carrying orders, rallying the men, and by every means in their power contributing to the success of the brigade.

Capt. Parshall was killed early in the action of the first day. He was a brave, noble soldier, an upright gentleman, and carries with him to the grave the love and regret of many friends.

Capt. Thoenssen was missing the evening of the second day, and I believe was captured. Captains Beatty and Cilley had each two horses shot under them.

There are many names particularly commended for courage and good behaviour, for which I respectfully refer to the reports of the regiments and the battery.

We have lost many gallant officers and men, a list of whom is herewith furnished you.

In the charge made by the 9th Ohio on the 19th which recaptured the battery of the regular brigade, their loss in killed and wounded was over fifty.

I am, Captain, very respectfully,
Your obedient servant,
(Signed)   F. VAN DERVEER,
Col. com'd'g 3rd brigade.

Official copy:
   JAMES W. WOOD,
     1st Lt. and Adjutant, 2d Minnesota vols.

[No. 20.]

COLONEL JAMES GEORGE RECOMMENDED FOR PROMOTION.

(Official Files, Adjutant General's Office, State of Minnesota.)

HEADQUARTERS 3D BRIGADE, 3D DIVISION, 14TH A. C.
CHATTANOOGA, TENN., Oct. 9th, 1863.

To the President of the United States:

SIR:—I respectfully recommend to your favorable consideration the name of Col. James George, commanding 2nd Minnesota Volunteers, for a commission as Brigadier General of Volunteers.

Col. George is the senior Colonel in the service from his State, and has by his conduct in the late battles proved that he is worthy of promotion. His regiment is remarkable for its steadiness, reliability and efficiency in action, which is attributable to his own coolness and intrepidity.

Very respectfully, your obedient servant,
(Signed)   F. VAN DERVEER,
Col. Com'd'g Brigade.

(*Endorsements.*)

HEADQUARTERS 3D DIVISION, 14TH A. C., D. C.
CHATTANOOGA, TENN., Oct. 9, 1863.

I cordially endorse the recommendation of Col. Van Derveer in this case. Col. George's conduct in command of his regiment came under my personal observation in the battles of the 19th and 20th September, at "Chattanooga," in which he displayed great bravery and coolness, and kept his regiment in admirable order during the fight of both days.

(Signed)   J. M. BRANNAN,
Brig. Gen. Com'd'g Division.

HEADQUARTERS 14TH ARMY CORPS.
CHATTANOOGA, TENN., Oct. 10, 1863.

Col. James George has commanded the 2nd Minnesota Volunteers for more than eighteen months, this regiment has always been regarded as one of the best in the service, and has always been commanded by him with ability, shows that he is worthy of promotion. I therefore cordially unite in the above recommendation.

(Signed)   GEO. H. THOMAS,
Maj. Gen. U. S. V.

HEADQUARTERS DEPARTMENT OF THE CUMBERLAND,
Oct. 12, 1863.

Col. George deserves the promotion asked, and I hope he will receive it.

(Signed)   W. S. ROSECRANS,
Maj. Genl.

[No. 21.]

(See regimental report of Mission Ridge in chapter ix of narrative.)

BATTLE OF MISSION RIDGE.

List of the killed and wounded, Second Regiment, Minnesota Volunteers.

(*Official Files, Adjutant General's Office, State of Minnesota.*)

COMPANY "A."

1st Lieut. Levi Ober.................Wounded slightly.
Corpl. A. J. Bolsinger.............   "   "
Private Chas B. Rouse..........   "   severely.
   "   Richard Rice..............   "   slightly.
   "   Adam Mann................   "   "

COMPANY "B."

Sergt. John Westerman.......... Killed.
" Benjamin P. Talbot...... Wounded mortally, since died.

COMPANY "C."

Private Rincis DeGrave.......... Wounded mortally, since died.
" Samuel S. Kline.......... " severely.
" Riley Barnhaus.......... " slightly.

COMPANY "D."

1st Lieut. Samuel G. Trimble.. Killed.
Corpl. John S. Mullen............ Wounded severely.
Private Joseph E. LeBlond..... " "
" Jesse M. Williams....... " slightly.
" Alexander Landrie..... " "

COMPANY "E."

2nd Lieut. Thos. G. Scott....... Wounded slightly.
Sergt. Holder Jacobus............ " "
" Thomas Harney.......... " "
Corpl. N. C. Rukkee............... " severely.
" Thomas Fowble.......... " slightly.
" O. P. Renne................ " "
Private J. L. Henningson....... " "
" Ole Hendrickson......... " "

COMPANY "H."

Private Samuel Loudon.......... Killed.
2nd Lieut. Thos. G. Quayle..... Wounded severely.
Private James Pelkey.............. " mortally, since died.
" William Gleason......... " severely.
" Isaac Sherman... .... " slightly.

COMPANY "I."

Corpl. J. Ira Tillotson............. Wounded severely.
Private Stephen W. Miller...... " slightly.
" Henry White............... " "
" Ethan A. Hitchcock.... " "

COMPANY "K."

Corpl. Henry F. Koch............ Killed.
Private George F. Lamphear.. "
1st Sergt. A. H. Reed............ Wounded severely.
Sergt. T. H. Pendergast.......... " slightly.
Private Philetus S. Barnett.... " severely.
" Wm. B. C. Evans........ " "
" Christian Kasmier...... " "

RECAPITULATION.

Officers killed 1	Officers wounded............. 3
Enlisted men killed.............4	Enlisted men wounded......31
Total killed.....................5	Total wounded...............34
Total killed and wounded................................39	
Total No. of officers and men engaged.....................185	

          J. W. BISHOP,
           Lt. Col. Com'd'g.

Paul Caviezel, Sergt. Company "F," wounded Oct. 5, died Oct. 22, '63.

Peter Peterson, private Company "E," wounded Oct. 12, died Oct. 13, '63.

[No. 22.]

BATTLE OF MISSION RIDGE.

Supplementary report by Lt. Col. J. W. Bishop.

(Official Files, Adjutant General's Office, State of Minnesota.)

HEADQUARTERS SECOND REGIMENT MINN. VOLS.
CHATTANOOGA, TENN., Dec. 10, 1863.

CAPT. JOHN R. BEATTY, A. A. A. G. 2nd Brig., 3rd Div., 14th A. C.:

CAPTAIN:—For the purpose of placing on record the names of the officers and men of my command who by gallant and meritorious conduct under fire, during the assault on Mission Ridge on the 25th ult., have entitled themselves to special mention, I respectfully submit the following report as supplementary to the general report already on file in your office.

There were present and engaged on that occasion one hundred and seventy enlisted men of the regiment and the following named officers, every one of whom is entitled to creditable mention.

Adjutant............................	James W. Wood.
Assistant Surgeon...............	Wm. Brown.
Captains............................	C. S. Uline.
"	J. C. Donahower.
"	John Moulton.
"	Levi Ober.

1st Lieutenants..........................Tenbroeck Stout,
    "   ....H. K. Couse, com'd'g his Co.,
    "   ....S. G. Trimble,
    "   ....W. W. Wilson, com'd'g his Co.,
    "   ....L. A. Holmes, com'd'g his Co.
2d Lieutenants ....T. G. Scott,
    "   ....John C. Jones,
    "   ....Edw. L. Kenny,
    "   ....Thos. G. Quayle.

To Capt. C. S. Uline, the senior of his grade in the regiment, was assigned the command of the two companies deployed to cover the formation and advance of the brigade in taking position for the assault; this duty was skilfully discharged, and in the furious assault and in the melee on the ridge he especially distinguished himself by his gallant example and by his coolness and promptitude in directing the enthusiasm of those who followed him.

1st Lieutenant Samuel G. Trimble, a gallant and faithful officer, was shot dead in the extreme front of the fight on the ridge. Beloved and respected by his comrades in life, his death in the very moment of victory cast a cloud over our thanksgiving for the triumph for which he gave his life.

2nd Lieut. Thomas G. Quayle fell at the head of his men in the melee on the ridge, severely wounded in the right knee.

Color Sergeant Holder Jacobus of Company "E" crossed lances with a rebel color sergeant over a Napoleon gun on the ridge, and for a moment the two disputed its possession. Only for a moment, however, and the gun with its mate was ours. Sergeant Jacobus was soon afterward wounded, and all of his guard save one were either killed or wounded.

1st Sergeant Alex. H. Reed commanded his company ("K") during the engagement, behaving with marked coolness and courage. He was severely wounded near the close of the fight on the ridge.

1st Sergeant George W. Shuman, of Company "I," distinguished himself by gallant conduct during the engagement, especially by taking the colors of the regiment from Corporal Mullen who had fallen wounded, and keeping them aloft and in front through the hottest of the fight.

Sergeant Lafayette Hadley of Company "B," Thos. Harney of Company "E," and A. B. White of Company "K," are all entitled to special notice for gallantry, as are also privates Cox, Marsh and McNeal and many others, whose gallant deeds, though telling in the fight, were not especially observed and reported.

I am, Captain, very respectfully,
Your most obedient servant,
(Signed) J. W. BISHOP, Lt. Col.,
Com'd'g 2nd Minn. Vols.

[No. 23.]

BATTLE OF MISSION RIDGE.

Report of Col. F. Van Derveer, commanding Brigade.

(*Official Files, Adjutant General's Office, State of Minnesota.*)

HEADQUARTERS 2D BRIGADE, 3D DIVISION, 14th A. C.
CHATTANOOGA, TENN.

CAPT. A. C. McCLURG, A. A. A. Gen'l, etc.:

CAPTAIN:— I have the honor to report the part taken by the 2d Brigade in the late engagements in front of Chattanooga.

My command consisted of the 9th Ohio Vols., Col. G. Kammerling; the 75th Indiana, Col. M. S. Robinson; the 87th Indiana, Col. Newell Gleason; the 105th Ohio, Lt. Col. W. B. Tolles; 101st Indiana, Lt. Col. Thos. Doan; 2d Minnesota, Lt. Col. J. W. Bishop; and the 35th Ohio, Lt. Col. H. V. N. Boynton; numbering in all 102 commissioned officers and 1,577 enlisted men.

Having been supplied with one hundred rounds of ammunition to the man, on the afternoon of the 23d of November I moved to a position three-quarters of a mile in front of Fort Phelps with my brigade formed in two lines, the left resting upon the Moore road and the right near General Turchin's Brigade. Here we remained in line with a strong picket in front until 8 o'clock A. M.; on the 25th, when in pursuance to orders from the General commanding the division, I deployed one regiment (35th Ohio) along my front and advanced it near without opposition—the enemy's pickets having been withdrawn about daybreak that morning, and several small parties left for observation retiring in haste on our approach. Afterwards this regiment was ordered to join the brigade, when the division was moved to the left to and beyond Calico Creek, crossing it near its mouth. Passing but a short distance from this creek an order came to countermarch, and we returned and took position about half a mile north of Bald Hill, facing, and twelve hundred yards distant from Missionary Ridge.

At this point I formed my brigade in two lines: The first composed of the 87th Indiana on the right; the 101st Indiana on the left, and the 35th Ohio in the centre. The second line was formed by the 75th Indiana, and 105th and 9th Ohio regiments. The 2nd Minnesota was placed in front of the brigade, with two companies under Capt. Uline, deployed as skirmishers, and the residue of the regiment behind them as a reserve.

I ordered my skirmishers to advance to the edge of the woods, examine the position of the enemy and report their apparent strength in and about the rifle pits at the foot of the ridge.

After remaining in this place for an hour, I was ordered to move forward and take the rifle pits; this was about 4 o'clock P. M.

I sent word to Lt. Col. Bishop to move at once with his skirmishers and reserve, and pushed up the brigade to keep within supporting distance. The rifle pits in our front appeared to be occupied by two battalions of the enemy, two stands of colors being visible upon their works. The skirmishers advanced gallantly into the open field, and under a heavy fire from the enemy's artillery on the ridge and musketry from the lower works, dashed forward at a double-quick without firing a shot. As they approached within one hundred and fifty yards of the enemy, great uneasiness was apparent among the men in the rifle pits, and by the time our skirmishers were at a distance of one hundred yards, they were retreating precipitately up the ridge to their rear. Lt. Col. Bishop immediately got his command under cover of the enemy's works, and within five minutes of this time my first line, having passed the open space under a very heavy, direct and enfilading fire from the enemy's batteries on the ridge, were also under cover of the same works. In the meantime my second line was brought forward into the open ground and the men ordered to lie down.

Fifteen minutes after the rifle pits were taken the General commanding the division ordered a charge upon the crest of the ridge. My brigade moved at once with cheers and a hearty good will, the 2nd Minnesota occupying a position in the first line. The precipitous ascent, the enemy's sharpshooters in front and the terrific enfilading artillery fire upon each flank, were forgotten in their eager haste to storm the heights. My second line came forward at a run, and after a few moment's rest at the foot of the ridge, followed closely the advance. In fifteen minutes more our colors were upon the summit, and in twenty minutes the rebels had been driven out of their works on the crest, and we occupied the ground in front of the brigade.

As my men sprang over the works, the enemy's cannoniers were caught in the act of loading, and were bayonetted or driven off before they could fire their pieces. Five guns were found here in position and captured by the brigade, two (2) by the 2nd Minnesota and three (3) by the 35th Ohio. The larger part of the enemy retired along the ridge towards the left, vigorously pursued and driven near half a mile.

For thirty minutes a very determined resistance was made by the enemy. Many of the troops of my command having in the charge up the ridge lost their regimental organization, were in some disorder for a short time, but all pressed towards the enemy. The 9th Ohio and 75th Indiana came up in good order and were placed in line perpendicular to the ridge and fronting the rebels. Darkness coming on, firing ceased on both sides, and my brigade bivouacked on the crest of Missionary Ridge.

After the action one other piece of artillery abandoned by the enemy was found by the 75th Indiana and taken charge of.

The guns that were captured by my command were left where found while our men pursued the enemy along the ridge towards Tunnel Hill. While they were thus absent the pieces were hauled off to our rear by men said to belong to Brig. Gen. Wood's division, which was upon our right. I saw these guns being taken towards the ground occupied by that division, and upon inquiry I was informed that they were being taken to a position where they could be used against the enemy. My brigade at the same time captured one caisson with six horses attached, and a limber with one pair of horses; these two were taken to the rear with the guns.

No other troops were near this battery when taken,— the enemy were driven from it by my own men and we thus lost possession whilst gallantly engaging the retreating rebel force. The next day I moved with the rest of the division to McAfee's Church and the succeeding to Ringgold. We were not, however, actively engaged; and on the 29th marched back to our camp at Chattanooga.

My loss upon the 25th was 2 officers killed and 13 wounded; 20 enlisted men killed and 126 wounded.

In this action my brigade fully sustained the reputation it had won at Chickamauga. None flinched from their duty.

I particularly commend the conduct of Col. Kammerling. 9th Ohio, Col. Robinson, 75th Indiana, Col. Gleason, 87th Indiana, Lt. Col. Doan, 101st Indiana, Lt. Col. Bishop, 2nd Minnesota, and Lt. Col. Boynton, 35th Ohio. These officers discharged their duties coolly and ably. Lt. Col. Boynton was severely wounded early in this engagement, when the command of his regiment devolved upon Maj. Budd, who is entitled to much praise for the energy and skill he exhibited in leading his men up the ridge.

Especial credit is due Lt. Col. Bishop for the management of his regiment when skirmishing in front of the brigade, and the gallant manner in which his command carried the rifle pits at the foot of the ridge.

There were many line officers and enlisted men who deserve commendation for their gallantry; for their names I respectfully refer you to the reports of regimental commanders.

The members of my staff with me on the field were Capt. J. R. Beatty, A. A. Gen'l, Capt. C. A. Cilley, Brig. Inspector, Capt. W. R. Tuttle, Brig. Engineer, 1st Lieut. S. Fortner, Provost Marshall, 1st. Lt. S. D. Parsons, A. A. Quartermaster, and 1st Lt. C. B. Williams, A. D. C. They rendered me great service, and entitled themselves to praise for their gallant conduct.

    I am, Captain,
      Very respectfully, &c.,
    (Signed)   F. Van Derveer,
        Col. 35th O. V. I.,
         Com'd'g 2nd Brigade.

[No. 24.]
PROMOTIONS RECOMMENDED.

HEADQUARTERS 2D BRIGADE, 3D DIVISION, 14th A. C.
Vinings Station, Ga., July 14th, 1864.

Brig. Gen. Oscar Malmros, Adjt. Gen. State of Minnesota:

GENERAL:—I have the honor to recommend the following promotions in the 2nd Regiment Minnesota Volunteers now under my command and forming part of the brigade.
  I. Lt. Col. J. W. Bishop to be Colonel.
  II. Major Calvin S. Uline to be Lt. Colonel.
  III. Capt. Clinton A. Cilley to be Major.

The regiment now having received two detachments of recruits, numbers six hundred and ninety-five (695) men aggregate, which, with two hundred recruits, which I am informed are now on the way to join it, will entitle the officers so promoted to be mustered accordingly.

I take this opportunity to state that the 2nd Minnesota Veteran Volunteer Infantry is regarded as one of the very best organizations in the service, and that the above named officers are especially deserving of promotion for their efficiency and strict attention to duty. The good of the service and justice to these officers require that the regiment be filled to the minimum, in order that a full quota of field officers may be mustered.

I am, very respectfully,
Your most obedient servant,
N. GLEASON,
Col. Com'd'g 2d Brig., 3d Div., 14th A. C.

(*Endorsements.*)

HEADQUARTERS 3D, DIVISION, 14th A. C.
July 14th, 1864.

The within recommendations for promotion in the 2nd Minn. Vols. are fully concurred in, and speedy action in the several cases urged. For nearly a year these officers have served in my commands, and I know them to be competent and in every way worthy of promotion.

Respectfully forwarded,
A. BAIRD,
Brig. Gen. Com'd'g Division.

HEADQUARTERS 14th A. C.
July 14th, 1864.

Respectfully forwarded. The propriety of these promotions is unquestionable, and they are earnestly recommended.

JOHN M. PALMER,
Maj. Gen. Com'd'g 14th A. C.

HEADQUARTERS DEPARTMENT OF THE CUMBERLAND.
July 15th, 1864.

Respectfully forwarded to his excellency the Governor of Minnesota, recommending that the promotion be made as requested of Lt. Col. Bishop, Major Uline and Capt. Cilley.

GEO. H. THOMAS, Maj. Gen. Com'd'g,
Dept. of the Cumberland.

[No. 25.]

ATLANTA CAMPAIGN.

(*Official Files, Adjutant General's Office, State of Minnesota.*)

List of casualties in the Second Regiment Minnesota Volunteer Infantry during the three months ending Aug. 6, 1864:

Name.	Rank and Co.		Date.	
John C. Jones	2d Lieut	B	June 18, 1864	Killed.
Peter G. Wheeler	Sergt. Maj. N. C. S.	"	22,	"
Spencer Lavicount	Private	F	" 22,	"
Nicholas Roppert	Corporal	G	" 18,	"
Charles F. Meyer	Captain	G	May 14,	" Wounded.
Samuel A. Field	Private	D	June 1,	"
Joseph Orcutt	Corporal	C	" 5,	"W'd and c'd.
David J. Bumgarner	Private	A	" 14,	" Wounded.
Roswell Ingalls	"	K	" 18,	"
Nelson Shelafoo	"	H	" 18,	"
Isaac Sherman	"	H	" 18,	"
Geo. Hetherington	"	H	" 18,	"
Henry Clinton	"	I	" 18,	"
Ira Holliday	"	J	" 18,	"
Francis Waldron	"	B	" 18,	"
James Whiting	"	B	" 18,	"
Squire Hoff	"	F	" 18,	"

Name.	Rank and Co.		Date.	
Wm. Bingham	Private	C	June 18, 1864	Wounded.
Martin V. Barber	"	K	" 19, "	Mortally.
Geo. Rutherford	Sergt.	F	" 19, "	Wounded.
Thomas Rutherford	"	D	" 20, "	"
Nicholas Sons	Corporal	E	" 20, "	"
Geo. Ainsworth	Sergt.	F	" 22, "	"
Wm. Madden	Corporal	F	" 22, "	"
James Thornton	Private	F	" 22, "	"
Frank Harris	"	F	" 22, "	"
Chas. F. Heyward	"	F	" 22, "	"
John E. Colburn	"	A	" 22, "	"
Lewis Horst	"	E	" 26, "	"
Thaddeus O'Kibben	"	E	May 20, "	"
Joseph Burger	"	H	July 9, "	"

Station—near Atlanta, Ga.
Date—Aug. 26th, 1864.
   (Signed)   J. W. BISHOP,
      Lt. Col. Com'd'g 2nd Minn.

Charles Jung, private Co. G, Sept. 1, wounded (Jonesboro).

George Adams, private Co. C, Sept. 1, wounded, (Jonesboro).

W. J. Johnson, private Co. C, Sept. 1, wounded, (Jonesboro).

[No. 26.]

Complimentary Letter from Brig. Gen. A. Baird, Com'd'g Division, to Gov. Miller.

(Certified copy in possession of J. W. B.)

HEADQUARTERS 3D DIVISION, 14TH A. C.
SAVANNAH, GA., January 6, 1865.

HIS EXCELLENCY, S. MILLER, Governor of Minnesota:

SIR,—In consequence of a letter addressed by you to Maj. Gen. Thomas, commanding the Army of the Cumberland, in which you promise to fill up the 2nd Reg. Minn. Vols. from the supplementary draft to be made in your state in November past, and ask that an officer be sent to receive the men, I have detailed Major Uline for that duty, with orders to report to you at St. Paul.

I trust that the condition of affairs may be such as to enable you to carry out the design which you expressed in your letter, and that Maj. Uline may soon return with the number of men required to fill up his ranks.

This regiment has been under my command for more than a year, and has won for itself, and for the soldiers of your state, a high reputation. It is one of the very best regiments in any of our armies, and I am sure that your men now entering the service cannot do more for the honor of their state, or serve with greater profit to themselves, than by becoming attached to it.

The three officers holding your commissions for the highest positions in the regiment are all men of remarkable merit, yet they are still serving in subordinate grades for want of the number of men required to muster them. They are Lt. Col. Bishop, Maj. Uline and Capt. Moulton, and all of them have earned their promotion many times since they have been under my command.

I am, sir, most respectfully,
Your obedient servant,
A. BAIRD,
Brig. Gen. Com'd'g Div.

[No. 27.]

SAVANNAH TO GOLDSBORO.

Report of Casualties, &c., to March 23d, 1865.

(Official Files, Adjutant General's Office, State of Minnesota.)

HEADQUARTERS 2D MINNESOTA VOLUNTEERS,
GOLDSBORO, N. C., March 23, 1865.

COL. OSCAR MALMROS, Adjt. Gen'l, State of Minnesota:

COLONEL,—I have the honor to report the 2d Minnesota Vol. Inf. at this place on the 23d inst. Having just received our back mail for sixty days we are overwhelmed with business, and a formal or detailed account now is out of the question.

Our monthly returns for January, February and March will be made and forwarded as soon as we can procure the blanks.

Our casualty list is hereto appended, and the following items may interest those who are interested in the regiment.

The number of miles marched from Savannah, Ga., January 20th, to Goldsboro, March 23d, not including foraging or work on wagon roads, or in the destruction of railroads, was four hundred and eighty. Much of it was done in bad weather and on bad roads, and not a little of it by night.

The number of serviceable horses and mules captured and turned in by the regiment was thirty.

During the campaign we drew from the trains one third rations of hard bread, coffee and sugar; all other supplies were foraged from the country along the line of march. Our aggregate number present when we marched from Savannah on the 20th of January was 526. Decrease during the campaign of 63 days was:

Men sent to general field hospital.................. 11
Missing, supposed to be captured....................... 5

Total decrease being about three per cent.

Aggregate present on arriving at Goldsboro, March 23, 510.

When I remember that about one-half of the men of the regiment are recruits of but a few months' service, and that the campaign has been one of the severest on record, the very small percentage of loss from the effective force is more than satisfactory to me.

I am equally grateful to the recruits (they may well drop that name now) for their patient and heroic endurance of privations and hardships to which they were little accustomed, and to the veterans who have so uniformly given a soldierly example to those of less experience in the rough ways of war.

We hope now to have a few days rest to obtain clothing and other much needed supplies, and having seven months' pay due us, a paymaster would find himself welcome here, too.

I am, very respectfully,
Your most obedient servant,
J. W. BISHOP, Lt. Col.
Com'd'g 2d Minn. Vol. Inf'y.

CASUALTY REPORT.

DIED.

Owen Lewis, Corporal..........Co. B...Feb.25, '65, of disease.

WOUNDED.

William S. Lyman, private.....Co. B...In action, March 20.
Christian Sanders, Sergt........Co. G...In action, March 20.

MISSING, SUPPOSED TO BE CAPTURED.

Isaac A. Peterson, private......Co. C...March 2d.
Mars Oleson, private..............Co. C...March 23d.
Sylvanus Stone, private.........Co. C...March 3d.
Ferdinand Birck, private........Co. F...February 12.
Thos. H. Garretson, private...Co. F...February 12.

J. W. BISHOP, Lt. Col.
Com'd'g 2d Minn. Vol. Inf'y.

[No. 28.]

PROMOTION ANNOUNCED.

HEADQUARTERS 3D DIV., 14th A. C.
June 13th, 1865.

LT. COL. C. S. ULINE, Com'd'g 2d Reg. Minn. Vols.:

COLONEL,—I have the honor to inform you that I have this day received from the Honorable Secretary of War, a letter of appointment as "Brigadier General of Volunteers by Brevet." (Commission dated April 9, 1865).

As I have never had permanently any other command than that of the regiment of which I have been for nearly four years a member, I desire to say through you that I attribute this complimentary promotion entirely to the gallant and soldierly conduct of the officers and men of that regiment, and that I tender to them my sincere thanks for the honor they have won for themselves and for me.

I am, very respectfully,
Your most obedient servant,
J. W. BISHOP, Col. 2d Minn. Vols.
Brevt. Brig. Gen'l U. S. V.

[No. 29.]

PROMOTION RECOMMENDED.

HEADQUARTERS 14th A. C.
SAVANNAH, GA., January 12, 1865.

Adjutant General U. S. A.:

SIR,—I have the honor to apply for the promotion by Brevet of the following named officers who have served with distinction in the campaign against Atlanta and Savannah:

* * * * * * * *

Lt. Col. J. W. Bishop, 2d Minn. Vol. Inf'y.

These officers have not only commanded their troops with uniform gallantry, but by their constant devotion to duty and attention to all the details and necessities of their commands, have brought them to a state of efficiency which entitles them to some recognition of their services.

I have the honor to be,
Very respectfully,
Your obedient servant, &c.,
JEF. C. DAVIS,
Brevt. Maj. Gen. Com'd'g.

HEADQUARTERS LEFT WING, ARMY OF GEORGIA.
SAVANNAH, GA., Jan'y 12, '65.

Respectfully forwarded, approved.

H. W. SLOCUM,
Maj. Gen. Com'd'g.

SECOND RECOMMENDATION.

HEADQUARTERS 14TH A. C.
WASHINGTON, D. C., May 29, 1865.

BRIG. GEN. L. THOMAS, Adjt. Gen. U. S. Army, Washington, D. C.:

I have the honor to report that on the 12th of January last I recommended Lt. Col. Bishop, of the 2d Minn. Vet. Vols., to the Department for promotion to the grade of Brigadier General by Brevet. Since that time this officer has been commissioned by the Governor of his state, Colonel of his regiment, and as such mustered. I desire respectfully to again ask the attention of the Department to the merits and claims of Col. Bishop and to renew the recommendation.

I am, very respectfully,
JEF. C. DAVIS,
Brvt. Maj. Gen. Com'd'g.

HEADQUARTERS ARMY OF GEORGIA.
Near WASHINGTON, D. C., May 30, 1865.

Respectfully forwarded to the Adjutant General of the Army, approved.

H. W. SLOCUM,
Maj. Gen'l Com'd'g.

[No. 30.]

Regiment Reported Ready for Discharge by Gen. J. W. Bishop, Commanding Brigade.

(Original document in possession of J. W. B.)

HEADQUARTERS 1ST BRIG., 3D DIV., 14TH ARMY CORPS.
LOUISVILLE, KY., July 8th, 1865.

BREV'T COL. A. C. MCCLURG, A. A. G. and Chief of Staff, 14th A. C.:

COLONEL,—Lt. Col. C. S. Uline, commanding 2d Regt. Minn. Vet. Vol. Inf'y, reports that regiment ready, and to be mustered for discharge tomorrow—the 9th.

I have therefore the honor to request that I may be ordered to assume command of and to report it to chief mustering officer at Fort Snelling, Minn., for discharge and final payment.

In making this application, permit me to say that as the time draws near when we are to leave the comrades we have so long served with, there are few, if any, who do not find that the joy and pride that we feel in the knowledge that our redeemed country no longer needs our service in the field, is mingled with a sadness that always attends the breaking up of long wonted associations.

Identified with the fortunes of the 14th Corps from its organization, and in it the only representative of the State that sent us to the field, it has been equally our care and our pride as a regiment, that Minnesota should never blush for the 14th Corps, and that the 14th Corps should never droop its laurels with shame at the name of Minnesota.

With the most grateful remembrance of the soldierly courtesy with which we have been uniformly treated by our comrades in arms from other states of the same, our own, country, I desire especially to acknowledge the kindly interest in the regiment which has been so often manifested by the Generals commanding the Division and the Corps.

I am, Colonel, very respectfully,
Your most obedient servant,
J. W. BISHOP,
Col. 2d Minn. Vols.,
and Brv't. Brig. Gen. Com'd'g Brigade.

[No. 31.]

Farewell Letter from Headquarters of 14th Army Corps, Gen. Jeff. C. Davis, Com'd'g.

(Official document in possession of J. W. B.)

HEADQUARTERS 14TH ARMY CORPS,
LOUISVILLE, KY., July 9, 1865.

GENERAL,—I have the honor to enclose to you a copy of the order relieving your regiment from the Corps and directing you to report it at Fort Snelling.

Until the time of separation came, none knew how strong were the attachments formed during the months and years of association in hardships and dangers as soldiers. His relations to the officers and men of the 2d Minnesota have always been a matter of pride and satisfaction to the Corps Commander, and from no regiment in the corps will he part with a deeper regret. He thanks one and all of the members of the organization for the constancy and devotion which have always marked their attention to the duties and requirements of soldiers in camp and on the march as well as on the field of action.

He congratulates you that your labors, hardships and dangers are over, and that with a country restored to peace and prosperity—partly through your exertions and sacrifices, you return once more to your homes.

None have a better record for discipline and drill and all the minutiæ of soldierly conduct as well as uniform gallantry on every field of action in which they have been engaged than the 2d Minnesota, and your state owes you thanks for the uniformly faithful manner in which you have performed your share of the task allotted to the soldiers of the Union.

Very respectfully your obedient servant, &c.,

A. C. McClurg, Brvt. Col.,
A. A. G. and Chief of Staff.

Brvt. Brig. Gen. J. W. Bishop,
    Com'd'g 2d Minn. Vols.

[No. 32.]

Final Order to Report at Fort Snelling for Muster-Out.
(Original document in possession of J. W. B.)

Headquarters 14th Army Corps,
Louisville, Ky., July 9, 1865.

Special Orders, }
    No. 5.   }

(*Extract.*)

II. The 2d Minnesota V. V. Infantry having been mustered on muster-out rolls, in accordance with existing orders, Brvt. Brig. Genl. J. W. Bishop, Colonel of the regiment, is hereby at his own request relieved from command of the 1st Brigade, 3d Division, 14th A. C., and will proceed forthwith with his regiment to Fort Snelling, Minn., and there report it in accordance with provisions of General Orders, No. 94, (C. S.) A. G. O., to the Chief Mustering Officer of the State of Minnesota (or his assistant at that point) for final discharge.

By command of Brevet Major Jeff. C. Davis.

A. C. McClurg,
Asst. Adjt. Genl. and Chief of Staff.

Brvt. Brig. Genl. J. W. Bishop,
    Com'd'g 1st Brig., 3d Div., 14th A. C.

[No. 33.]

ROSTER OF COMMISSIONED OFFICERS.

In Service when the Regiment Departed for the South, October, 1861.

FIELD AND STAFF.

Colonel, Horatio P. Van Cleve; Lieutenant Colonel, James George; Major, Alexander Wilkin; Adjutant, Daniel Heaney; Quartermaster, W. S. Grow; Quartermaster Sergeant, S. D. Parsons; Sergeant Major, C. A. Cilley; Surgeon, R. H. Bingham; Assistant Surgeon, M. C. Tolman; Chaplain, T. R. Cressey.

Company A—Captain, Judson W. Bishop; 1st Lieut., Charles Haven; 2d Lieut., Charles H. Barnes.

Company B—Captain William Markham; 1st Lieut., Daniel Heaney; 2d Lieut., Abram Harkins.

Company C—Captain, Peter Mantor; 1st Lieut., Henry C. Simpson; 2d Lieut., David B. Bailey.

Company D—Captain, Horace H. Western; 1st Lieut., Moses C. Tuttle; 2d Lieut., Samuel P. Jennison.

Company E—Captain, Asgrim K. Skaro; 1st Lieut., E. St. Julian Cox; 2d Lieut., Jeremiah C. Donahower.

Company F—Captain, John B. Davis; 1st Lieut., David B. Loomis; 2d Lieut., John S. Livingston.

Company G—Captain, Andrew R. Kiefer; 1st Lieut., Jacob Mainzer; 2d Lieut., Fred A. Brandt.

Company H—Captain, Nelson W. Dickinson; 1st Lieut., John R. Beatty; 2d Lieut., Jerome Dame.

Company I—Captain, John Foote; 1st Lieut., William S. Grow; 2d Lieut., Calvin S. Uline.

Company K—Captain, J. J. Noah; 1st Lieut., Wm. W. Woodbury; 2d Lieut., Ephraim A. Otis.

[No. 34.]

ROSTER OF COMMISSIONED OFFICERS

At Re-Enlistment, Chattanooga, Tenn., January, 1864.

FIELD AND STAFF.

Colonel, James George, absent on sick leave; Lieut. Col., J. W. Bishop, Com'd'g; Major, John B. Davis; Adjutant, J. W. Wood; Quartermaster, S. D. Parsons; Surgeon, M. C. Tolman; Assistant Surgeon, Wm. Brown.

Company A—Captain, Levi Ober; 1st Lieut., Ed. Kenny.
Company B—Captain, Abram Harkins; 1st Lieut., W. W. Wilson; 2d Lieut., John C. Jones.
Company C—Captain, C. A. Cilley; 1st Lieut., H. K. Couse; 2d Lieut., Matthias Thoeny.
Company D—Captain, John Moulton; 1st Lieut., Hiram Lobdell.
Company E—Captain, J. C. Donahower; 1st Lieut., Augustus E. Alden; 2d Lieut., Thomas G. Scott.
Company F—Captain, David B. Loomis; 1st Lieut., John S. Livingston; 2d Lieut., Edward Wait.
Company G—Captain, C. F. Meyer; 1st Lieut., Henning V. Rumohr; 2d Lieut., Charles Rampe.
Company H—Captain, John R. Beatty; 1st Lieut., L. N. Holmes; 2d Lieut., Thomas G. Quayle.
Company I—Captain, C. S. Uline; 1st Lieut., Tenbroeck Stout.
Company K—Captain, W. W. Woodbury; 2d Lieut., D. S. Coverdale.

[No. 35.]

FINAL ROSTER OF COMMISSIONED OFFICERS

At Muster-out, July, 1865.

Colonel, Judson W. Bishop (Brvt. Brigadier General); Lieutenant Colonel, C. S. Uline; Major, John Moulton; Adjutant, F. S. Hoffstott; Surgeon, Wm. Brown; Chaplain, Levi Gleason; Quartermaster, J. L. Kenny; Sergeant Major, W. C. Wynkoop; Quartermaster Sergeant, W. C. Garrett; Commissary Sergeant, Samuel Bowler; Hospital Steward, Robert Bailey; Musician, R. G. Rhodes (leader of the band).

Company A—Capt. Ed. L. Kenny; 1st Lieut., A. Kalder; 2d Lieut., A. McCorkle.
Company B—Captain, J. W. Wood; 1st Lieut., J. L. Gaskill; 2d Lieut., F. Kelsey.
Company C—Captain M. Thoeny; 1st Lieut., W. H. Mills; 2d Lieut., J. P. Jackson.
Company D—Captain, G. W. Shuman; 1st Lieut., J. T. McCoy; 2d Lieut., J. W. Stuart.
Company E—Captain, T. G. Scott; 1st Lieut., B. F. Sylvester; 2d Lieut., T. D. Fowble.

Company F—Captain, J. S. Livingston; 1st Lieut., C. H. Friend; 2d Lieut., F. R. Harris.

Company G—Captain, H. V. Rumohr; 1st Lieut., A. G. Essen; 2d Lieut., F. Lambrecht.

Company H—Captain, L. N. Holmes; 1st Lieut., E. K. Wasser; 2d Lieut., Daniel Fagan.

Company I—Captain, T. Stout; 1st Lieut., E. V. Dickey; 2d Lieut., H. H. Hills.

Company K—Captain, D. S. Coverdale; 1st Lieut., A. H. Reed; 2d Lieut., A. B. White.

(Only three of these officers appear in the list of original commissioned officers.)

[No. 36.]

MEMORANDA.

Date of mustering the first two companies	June 26, 1861
Date of organization as a regiment	July 22, 1861
Date of re-muster in as veterans	Dec. 29, 1863
Date of final payment and discharge	July 20, 1865
Number of men mustered into the regiment	1,780
Number of men commissioned as officers	91
Number of men wounded in action	276
Of whom were killed or mortally wounded	68
Number of men died of diseases	167
Number of men discharged for disability	277
Number transferred or promoted out of the regiment	76
Number reported as deserted	61
Number of officers resigned	40
Number of men discharged at the end of three years' time, or at end of war and away from regiment	353
Number of men present at final discharge of regiment	699
Number of men on the rolls at the final muster out	821

It appears that of the whole number of men mustered into the regiment from first to last, about 15 per cent were wounded in battle, and about one fourth of these were killed or mortally wounded.

Nearly 9 per cent of the whole number died in the service of disease, and 15 per cent were discharged for disability; 4½ per cent were transferred or promoted out of the regiment, 3½ per cent deserted the service, and 2¼ per cent (officers) resigned for various reasons during the four years' service. Twenty per cent of the whole number were discharged at the expiration of the original years' enlistment, and at the close of the war but away from the regiment, and 40 per cent of the whole number were present in the regiment at its final muster out.

Of the thirty-seven commissioned officers who were in the regiment at the end of its service, only three were commissioned officers at the beginning; all the others (except the surgeon) had been promoted from the ranks.

While the regiment had various periods of encampment or post duty, it had considerable exercise on foot. In 1862, '63 and '64 it marched by the record 5,153 miles; an average of 4¾ miles a day, including Sundays, for the whole time. No record was kept for 1861 or 1865. It is believed, however, that the average daily marching in those years would exceed that for the years given.

[No. 37.]

RE-UNION OF 1887.

Letter from Colonel H. V. N. Boynton.

WASHINGTON, Aug. 11, 1887.

MY DEAR GENERAL BISHOP,—You may be sure I was glad to receive your invitation for the re-union of the Second Minnesota—of glorious deeds and memories. The historical pamphlet you sent me was one of the most welcome documents I ever received. For, aside from all that pertained to your own regiment, there was much which was common to all the comrades in the brigade. In fact, it is impossible to separate the history of the Second Minnesota, the Thirty-fifth Ohio, the Ninth Ohio and the Eighty-seventh Indiana. I am sure each is proud of the splendid record of the others. No doubt it has often occurred to you, as it has to me, that while many other brigades did all that could be done on many fields, it happened to few to have the record of ours in one respect. We had the peculiar good fortune to be never obliged either by the enemy or by the contingencies of movements on any field to give a foot of ground in the presence of the enemy. That is a heritage which we all share. It would give me keen pleasure to meet you again. Give an old comrade's love to the living veterans of your regiment. They may not remember me, but I have vividly and proudly in mind their splendid bearing at Chicamauga and Mission Ridge and other fields of their renown. I am sorry that I cannot attend the re-union; if it were possible, I would go. Believe me, dear General, with a thrill of the old times,

Cordially yours,
H. V. BOYNTON,
(Late Lt. Col. com'd'g 35th Ohio Vols.)

Telegram from Colonel Ferdinand VanDerveer.

HAMILTON, OHIO, Sept. 15, 1887.

To Gen. J. W. BISHOP:

I wish I could meet with the old boys of the Second Minnesota today. Their soldierly qualities were unsurpassed on the field of battle. I remember them as *the regiment without a straggler at Chicamauga*. Convey to them not only my profound respect but say in addition that my heart goes out to them. They deserve well of our country.

Very truly,
F. VANDERVEER,
(Late Col. 35th Ohio Vols., com'd'g Brigade.)

Letter from General A. Baird.

HOTEL CHATHAM, PARIS, Oct. 1st, 1887.

Gen. J. W. BISHOP:

MY DEAR GENERAL,—Your kind letter of Sept. 3d, inviting me to attend the re-union of the *surviving* members of the Second Minnesota Regiment on Sept. 15th, has been forwarded and has reached me here, where I have been to attend certain military maneuvers of French troops. It reached my hand too late for a reply to be read at the meeting, which I regret as well as not being able to be there myself.

The word "surviving" which you use is a sad one. Most of the men must have been younger than I, yet I survive, but to retire from active service next year. Every man of the Second Minnesota Regiment ought to feel proud that he belonged to it. I have known your regiment well, as you know. I have seen the soldiers of all countries, and I can truthfully say that I have never seen men that I would more willingly trust myself with in an hour requiring the highest strain on manhood and bravery, than those of the Second Minnesota.

With the warmest friendship for yourself and for the regiment,

Most truly yours,

A. BAIRD,

(Late Maj. Gen. com'd'g Division.)

Letter from General W. S. Rosecrans.

TREASURY DEPARTMENT, REGISTER'S OFFICE.

Sept. 6th, 1887.

J. W. BISHOP, ESQ.:

DEAR COMRADE,—I remember the Second Minnesota very well, and am a witness to their gallantry, patriotism and courage. I have good reason to remember it gratefully.

Please present my best wishes to the assembled comrades and tell them that, if duty permitted, I should enjoy nothing better than to be at the re-union in St. Paul on the 15th inst.

Since dictating the above, the pamphlet "Official Records" of the regiment has come to hand, and revives many lively memories of the Second's fighting and staying qualities. My warmest good wishes to each comrade of that regiment.

Very truly yours,

W. S. ROSECRANS.

(Late Maj. Gen. com'd'g Army of the Cumberland.)

www.ingramcontent.com/pod-product-compliance
Lightning Source LLC
Chambersburg PA
CBHW032138230426
43672CB00011B/2380